BUCK BROWN

Acquisition and editorial: *Nathaniel Gunod*

Editorial: *Michael Rodman*

Music Typesetting: *Gary Tomassetti*

Cover, CD and interior design: *Timothy Phelps*

CD Recorded and engineered by *Buck Brown, Washington, D.C.*

CD Mastered at Bar None Studio, Northford, CT

Cover photo: *Tim Becker/Creative Images*

Guitar courtesy of David Smolover

Book: ISBN 1-929395-34-5

Book and CD: ISBN 1-929395-35-3

CD: ISBN 1-929395-36-1

Table of Contents

Introduction 3

About the Author 4

Chapter 1—Alternate Picking 5
   Right-Hand Damping 5
   Finger Independence 7
   Eighth Notes Across the Fingerboard 8
   Eighth-Note Triplets Across the Fingerboard 12
   Combined Fingering Triplets
      Across the Fingerboard 16
   Shifting Eighth Notes Up the Fingerboard 17
   Chromatic Exercises 18
   Sliding Exercises 19
   F Major Modes—Two Notes Per String 20

Chapter 2—Hammer-Ons & Pull-Offs 22
   Double and Multiple Hammer-Ons 25
   Pull-Offs 26
   Double Pull-Offs 28
   Hammer-On/Pull-Off Combinations 29

Chapter 3—Scale Combinations 30
   More Scale Combinations 33
   Going Up and Down the Fingerboard Quickly 34

Chapter 4—Cross Picking,
String Skipping, Finger Rolls 38
   Arpeggio Patterns 38
   Major Linkages 41
   13th Arpeggios 43

Chapter 5—Sweeping, Rolling,
Double Stops, Octaves 45
   Sweeping Down 45
   Two-in-a-Row Sweeps 47
   Sweeping Up 48
   Rolling 49
   Double and Triple Stops 50
   Octaves 51

Chapter 6—Chords 53
   Anchor Fingers 56
   Multiple Anchor Fingers 57
   Shifting 58
   Stretching in Chords 60

Chapter 7—Comping 63
   Four to the Bar 63
   Pick and Fingers 65
   Two-Note Voicings 66
   Three-Note Voicings 67
   Parallel and Contrary Motion 68
   Counter Lines and Common Tones 69
   Pedal Tones 70
   Fingerstyle 72
   Harmonics 74

Track 01

A compact disc is available with each book of this series. Using these discs will help make learning more enjoyable and the information more meaningful. The CD will help you to play the correct notes, rhythms and feel of each example. The track numbers below the symbols correspond directly to the example you want to hear. Track 1 will help you tune to this CD.

Introduction

To become a better jazz guitar player, you need to spend some serious time "learning the moves"— the techniques that jazz guitarists employ and the little tricks of the trade that make them sound so good. You also have to understand jazz theory but that is not the purpose of this book. Here, we are concerned with technique— "chops," if you will.

This book is filled with exercises, each of which can help you with a specific technical issue. For example, if you have tried playing octaves and haven't been able to master the technique, you can learn the best ways to play octaves right here in this book. Even more specifically, there are lots of exercises designed solely to get your fretting-hand fingers to act independently, which is not something they do naturally. You have to train your fingers to act alone—to be able to do something while other fingers are doing something else.

This book also provides technical training for your picking hand. Alternate picking exercises, pick and fingers techniques and fingerstyle jazz playing are all looked at in detail. Also, there is an extensive look at chords— how best to move from one to another, what are the most common sets of strings on which chords are played, how to recognize and use anchor fingers and how to employ devices like contrary motion, counter lines, pedal tones and harmonics.

Technical training is challenging, and may even seem somewhat daunting. But with application on your part, and a willingness to work at each exercise until you absolutely have it under your fingers and understand it intellectually, you will become a much better player. Much of the material presented here is useable in jazz improvisation. As you play an exercise, see if you can determine where you might be able to use it in soloing. You will have to edit the exercise to make it presentable in a soloing context.

This book assumes you know how to read standard music notation but also provides tablature (TAB). It assumes you understand the basic musical ideas behind jazz already. It is not a jazz idea book that provides tips for playing jazz (for that, see *Jazz Skills* by Jody Fisher, also published by the National Guitar Workshop). Nor is it a method that teaches non-jazzers how to play jazz (for that, see Jody Fisher's *Complete Jazz Guitar Method*, published by the National Guitar Workshop and Alfred Publishing). *This book is about developing the physical skills required for playing jazz guitar.*

I hope this book helps you play cleaner, faster and better overall. The goal is, as always, no mistakes—just the joy of making music. See you at the gig.

About the Author

Buck Brown knows that guitar playing is the "real job" his mom always told him to get. In the past 35 years, he has been fortunate to play with such great artists as Nils Lofgren, Tony Trischka, Stacy Phillips, Dave Hamburger, Robert Lee Castleman, Mark Egan and all of the incredible teachers at the National Guitar Workshop (where he taught from 1984 to 1991). Buck has written ten National Guitar Workshop publications (under the name Robert Brown) including *Chord Connections*, his master work on guitar harmony.

As a composer, he has written music for innumerable episodes of *America's Most Wanted*, has won an Emmy Award in Cleveland, a Bronze Medal at the New York Film Festival and has been nominated twice for Helen Hayes Awards in Musical Theatre. When he is not on the road, Buck plays and teaches in Washington, D.C., is married to the fabulous chanteuse Rebecca Davis, lives with three dogs, bats right, throws right and plays loud.

Chapter 1

Alternate Picking

Alternate picking is the first technique that you must have in order to accomplish the smooth, articulated and fast playing we all strive for. The idea is to alternate *downstrokes* (⊓, towards the floor) and *upstrokes* (∨, towards the ceiling) with the pick in a clear, deliberate manner. Try to make your downstrokes sound just like your upstrokes, at least for now. Down the road, you will be able to make them sound differently when, and if needed. Keep in mind that, unless otherwise indicated, all exercises in this book are to be played with alternate picking.

Right-Hand Damping

The second technique you will have to learn is *right-hand damping*. It is important to eliminate the noise of unwanted ringing strings with your picking hand. Try laying the meaty part of your picking hand (the pinky side) against the lower strings as you play the higher strings. Try using your 2nd, 3rd and maybe even 4th fingers to stop the higher strings ringing when you are playing the lower strings. This takes lots of practice. Don't expect miracles the first time you try it. You will develop your own way to damp out the offending strings. The good news is that you are aware of the problem and, over time, you can solve it. Stay on top of it.

Now onto the first exercise which will start you on the path towards a great technique.

2

EXERCISE 1: ALTERNATE PICKING TREMOLO

Tremolo is a rapid repetition of a note or chord. Alternating downstrokes and upstrokes, play the following exercise slowly at first. Try to make every note even in terms of volume and *timbre* (tone color—the way that the note sounds). When you get to the end of the exercise, turn around and come back to the beginning (backwards) in the same way. As you gain confidence, gradually increase the tempo until you can play it quite rapidly. This is an *A Mixolydian Scale* (a major scale with a ♭7).

The numbers under the TAB are finger numbers. 1 is the index finger of the fretting hand, 4 is the pinky.

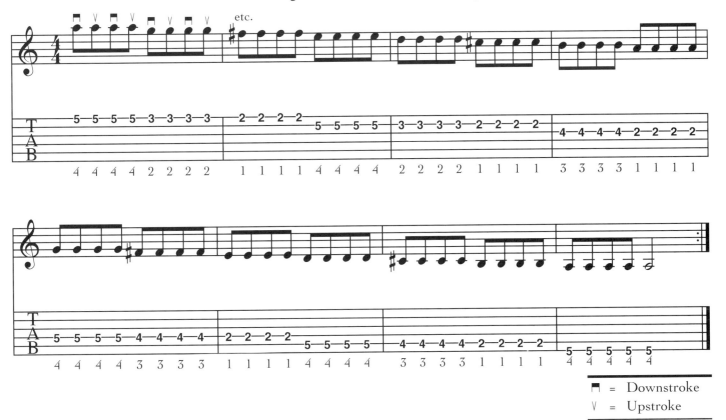

⊓ = Downstroke
∨ = Upstroke

EXERCISE 2: G BLUES PENTATONIC

Try this one with regular alternate picking (as in Exercise #1) and then try it with *reverse alternate picking*: upstroke, downstroke, upstroke, downstroke, etc.

EXERCISE 3: 4-3-2-1 DESCENDING AND 1-2-3-4 ASCENDING ALTERNATE PICKING

This one will help you learn how to time the left-hand movements with the right-hand alternate picking.

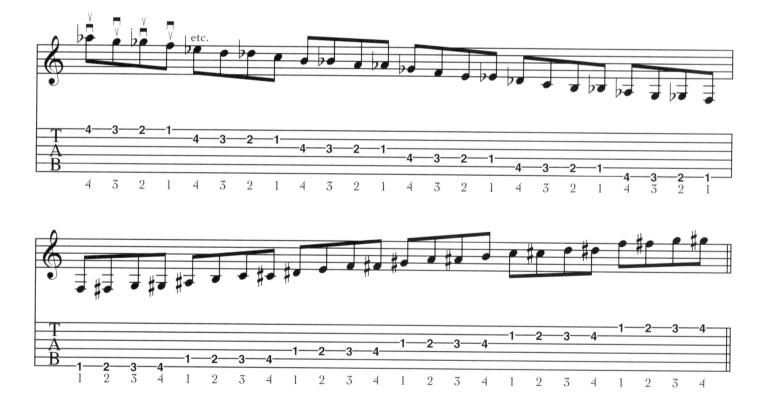

Finger independence—the ability to control the separate movements of the fingers—is one of the hardest mountains to climb as a guitar player. Fingers get tense and fly away from the fingerboard, and the movement of one finger may cause twitches in the others. This next exercise will help. Do it slowly. Don't forget your alternate picking.

 4   EXERCISE 4: ONE FINGER AT A TIME

Read the diagrams from left to right. The vertical lines are the strings, with the left-most line representing the 6th (lowest) string and the right-most line representing the 1st string. The horizontal lines are frets and the numbers to the left of the diagram tell us which frets they are. The numbers inside the circles are the finger numbers.

Move one finger at a time, holding fingers that have been placed down until their turn to move.

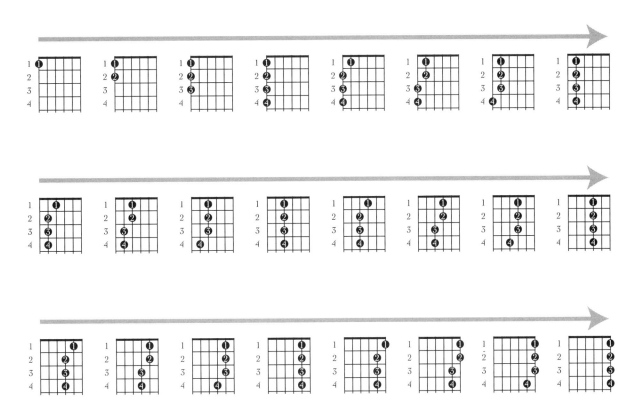

The following four pages of exercises have to do with two important technical issues: finger independence and speed. You will quickly see the patterns that are being set up in each exercise. The idea is to start with the 1st string and work your way across the fingerboard to the 6th string. Then turn around and come back up to where you started. The first twelve exercises work on pairs of fingers using important moves you will have to master. Don't forget to use alternate picking.

5.1   EXERCISE 5: 1-2

5.2   EXERCISE 6: 2-1

5.3   EXERCISE 7: 1-3

6.1

EXERCISE 8: 3-1

6.2

EXERCISE 9: 1-4

6.3

EXERCISE 10: 4-1

EXERCISE 11: 2-3

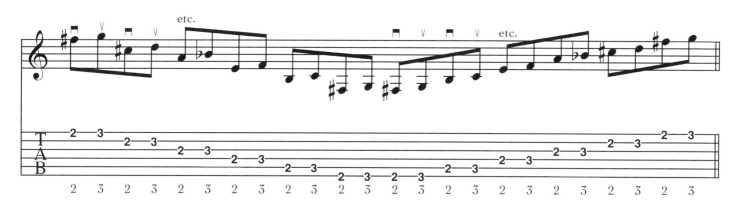

EXERCISE 12: 3-2

EXERCISE 13: 2-4

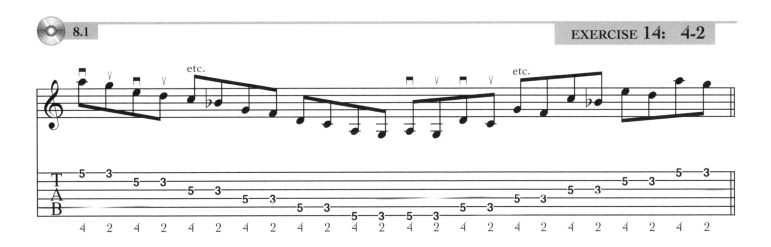

The next set of twelve exercises involves playing *eighth-note triplets* (three eighth notes in the time of two). Think of the three notes as being the three syllables of the word *"evenly"*. It will help if you say to yourself: *e-ven-ly, e-ven-ly, e-ven-ly, e-ven-ly* as you play these exercises. The hard part is remembering that, because you are playing three notes at a time, your alternate picking will become: downstroke/upstroke/downstroke – upstroke/downstroke/upstroke. Watch yourself closely and make sure you are doing this correctly. These exercises are also designed to strengthen your 3rd and 4th fingers, which are usually the weakest fingers.

9.1 **EXERCISE 17: 1-2-3**

9.2 **EXERCISE 18: 3-2-1**

9.3 **EXERCISE 19: 1-2-4**

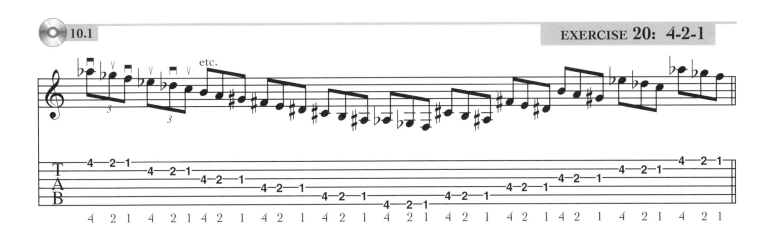

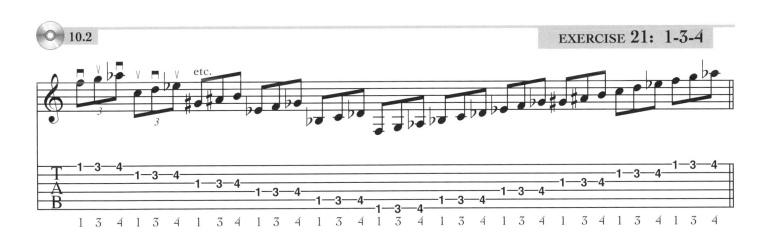

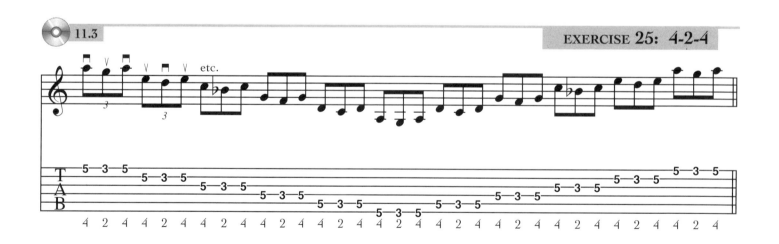

This last group of exercises on triplets combines some of those that we've been working on, which makes the whole exercise more difficult than the sum of its parts. Play slowly at first and remember to alternate pick.

13.1   **EXERCISE 29: COMBINED FINGERING 1**

13.2   **EXERCISE 30: COMBINED FINGERING 2**

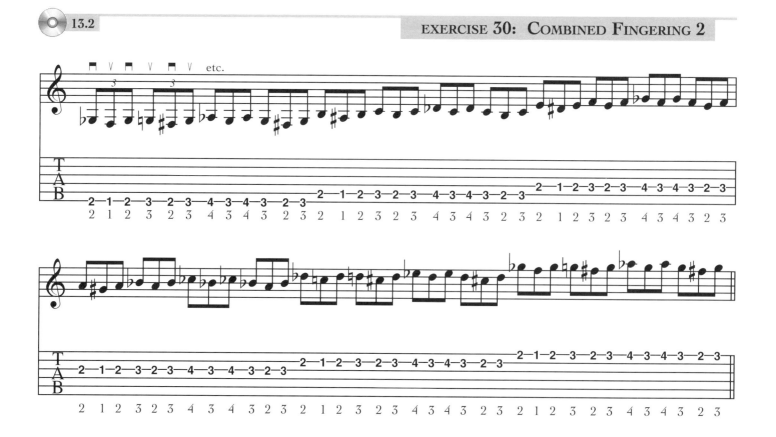

14.1

EXERCISE 31: 1-2-3-4, SHIFT 4-3-2-1

In Exercise #31, you will ascend the fingerboard on one string by playing 1-2-3-4 and then *shift* (move to a new position) your hand up one fret and descend, playing 4-3-2-1. Here it is written out on the 1st string. Get it going here and then do it on all six strings.

 14.2

EXERCISE 32: 1-2-3-4/1-2-3-4, SHIFT, 4-3-2-1/4-3-2-1

Exercise #32 is very similar to #31. The difference is that it covers two strings. It is shown below using the 2nd and 1st strings. As always, you should practice the exercise on the other string pairs: 3rd and 2nd, 4th and 3rd, 5th and 4th and 6th and 5th.

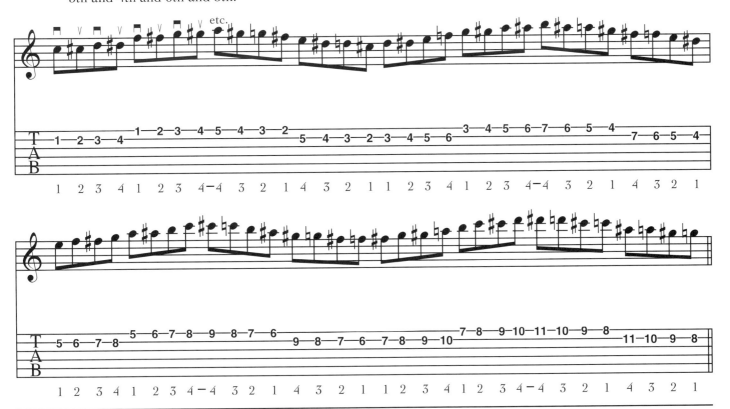

The first *chromatic* (a series of notes moving in half steps) exercise starts on the 6th string and, using open strings and fretted notes, works its way up to the 1st string. Don't get too comfortable with the pattern because it changes on the 3rd string and on the 1st string, there are two ascending shifts. Play this slowly enough so that a listener couldn't hear you change strings or shift positions. Also, this is a good opportunity to try some reverse alternate picking (up/down) as well as the normal down/up style.

15.1

EXERCISE 33: OPEN STRING CHROMATIC

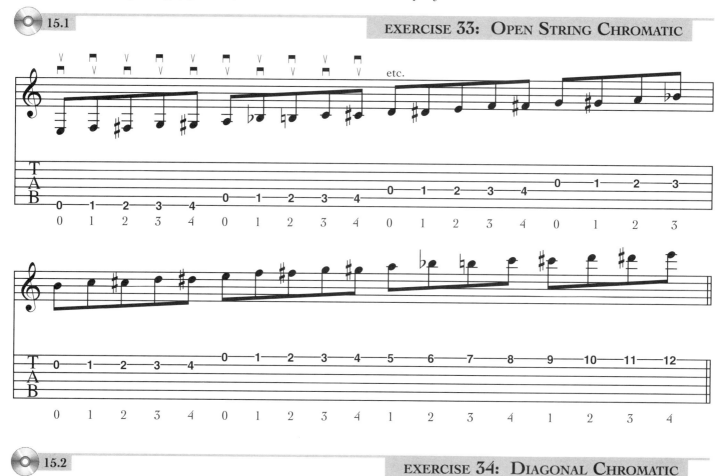

15.2

EXERCISE 34: DIAGONAL CHROMATIC

The following exercise starts in 5th position, with your 1st finger on the 5th fret of the 6th string. The finger pattern is 1-2-3-4 (ascending) 4-3-2-1 (descending). Each time you shift to another string, you shift down one fret (as you ascend from the 6th string to the 1st) or up one fret (as you descend from the 1st string to the 6th). The one exception to this is when moving between the 3rd and 2nd strings…no shift there.

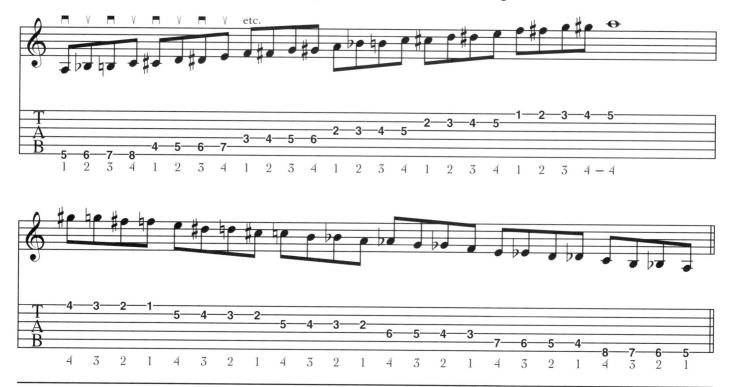

Jazz guitar players often *slide* from one position to another. Sliding is playing consecutive notes on the same string with the same finger. We must be able to slide on any finger or combination of fingers while moving up the fingerboard. The following exercises help you to do exactly that. Again, start slowly and work up to a hot tempo. And, of course, do each exercise on every string.

16.1 — **EXERCISE 35: SLIDING 1 AND 4**

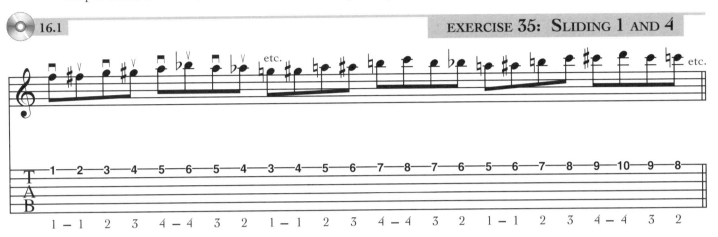

16.2 — **EXERCISE 36: SLIDING 2 AND 4**

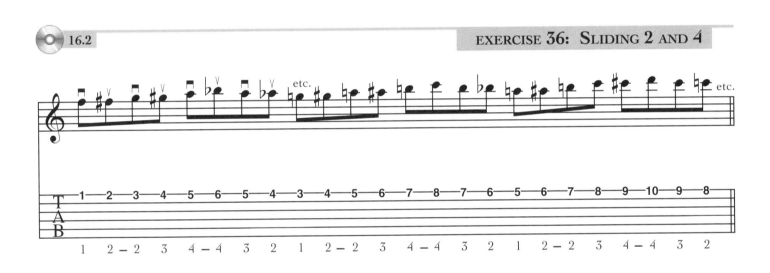

16.3 — **EXERCISE 37: SLIDING 3 AND 4**

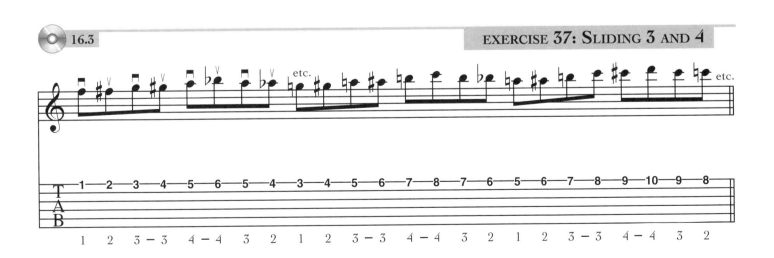

Here is a cool exercise that gets you using combinations of two fingers going across and up the fingerboard by modal position (think John McLaughlin). In this key, the scales are: F Ionian (major), G Dorian, A Phrygian, B♭ Lydian, C Mixolydian, D Aeolian and E Locrian. For a further discussion of modes, see *The Guitar Mode Encyclopedia* by Jody Fisher, published by the National Guitar Workshop and Alfred Publishing.

Learn each pattern, play through each scale slowly until you get the hang of it, and don't forget to use alternate picking.

17.1

EXERCISE 38: F IONIAN — TWO NOTES PER STRING

17.2

EXERCISE 39: G DORIAN — TWO NOTES PER STRING

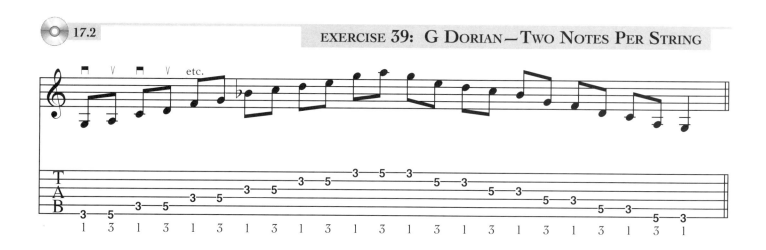

17.3

EXERCISE 40: A PHRYGIAN — TWO NOTES PER STRING

EXERCISE 41: Bb Lydian—Two Notes Per String

EXERCISE 42: C Mixolydian—Two Notes Per String

EXERCISE 43: D Aeolian—Two Notes Per String

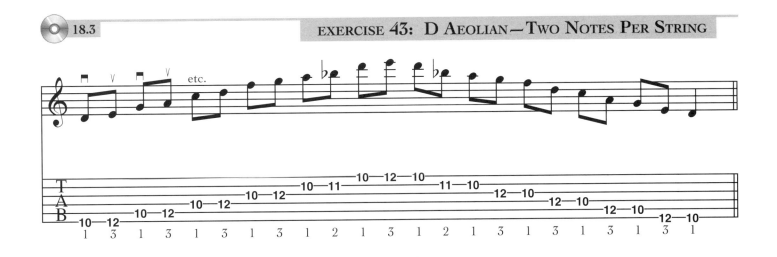

EXERCISE 44: E Locrian—Two Notes Per String

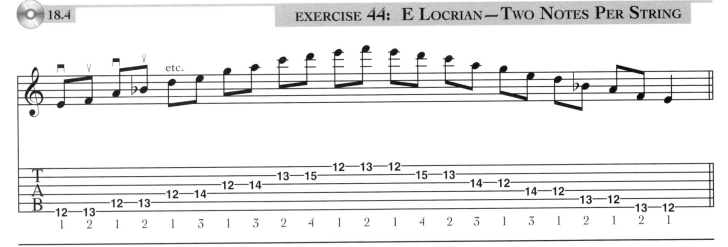

Chapter 2 Hammer-Ons & Pull-Offs

A *hammer-on* is an ascending *slur* (a curved line indicating that the notes should be played legato—smoothly with only one attack). This is accomplished by picking one note and then making a second note sound by hammering a finger down on a higher fret (and not plucking). Make sure that the hammered note has plenty of volume and good tone.

19

EXERCISE 45: HAMMER-ONS FROM OPEN STRINGS

20

EXERCISE 46: HAMMER-ONS WITH THE 1ST FINGER

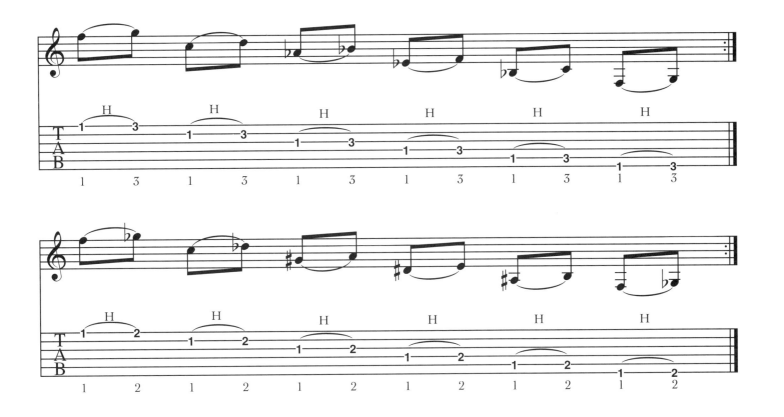

Often, you will be required to play hammer-ons while playing a chord. The next examples show some very common hammer-ons within chords. Make sure you can hear the hammered note or notes as part of the chord.

21   EXERCISE **47:** HAMMER-ONS INSIDE CHORDS

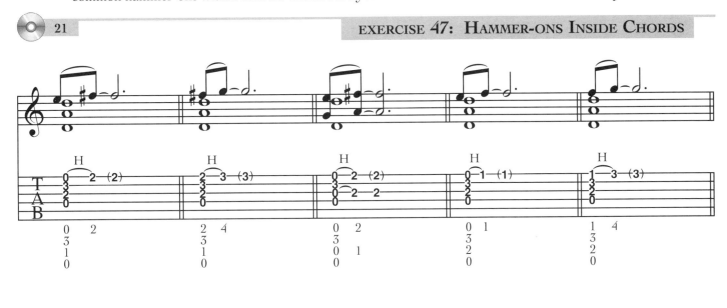

22   EXERCISE **48:** HAMMER-ONS INSIDE CHORDS

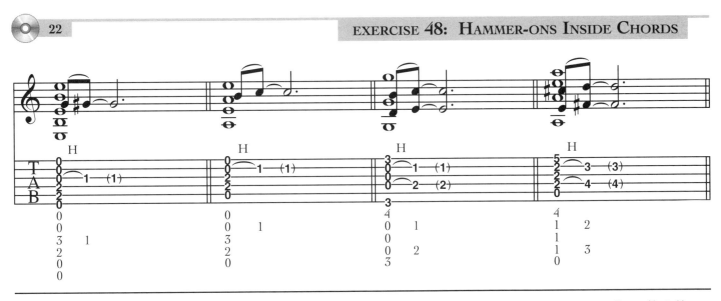

This exercise moves in minor 3rds up the fingerboard. The fingerings remain the same as the passage ascends. When you get to the top (C♭ to D♭), shift up one half step and then descend similarly.

23.1

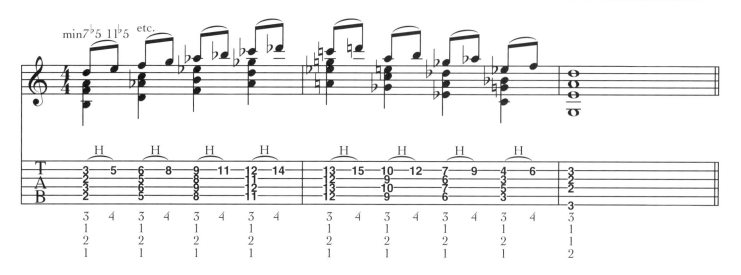

23.2

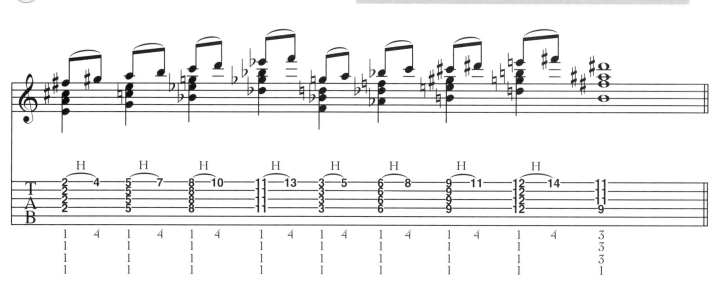

If you can do one hammer, you can do two or more in a row. Check it out. It's almost like rolling your fingers over the notes.

24.1

EXERCISE 51: DOUBLE HAMMER 1-2-4

24.2

EXERCISE 52: DOUBLE HAMMER 1-3-4

24.3

EXERCISE 53: TRIPLE HAMMER 1-2-3-4

Pull-offs are the opposites of hammer-ons. They are descending slurs. Pick a note and then, using a lot of pressure from your left-hand finger, literally pull the finger away from the string, in a downward direction (toward the floor), thus causing a lower pitch to sound. When not pulling-off to an open string, the lower finger must be in position before pulling off from the higher note. It is a wonderfully expressive technique and the following exercises will help you learn how to do it with every finger.

25.1

EXERCISE 54: 1ST FINGER PULL-OFF TO OPEN STRINGS

Now do the same exercise using your 2nd finger.

25.2

EXERCISE 55: 2ND FINGER PULL-OFF TO OPEN STRINGS

EXERCISE 56: 3RD TO 1ST FINGER PULL-OFFS

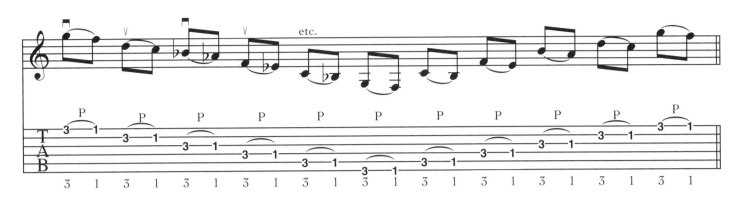

EXERCISE 57: 4TH TO 1ST FINGER PULL-OFFS

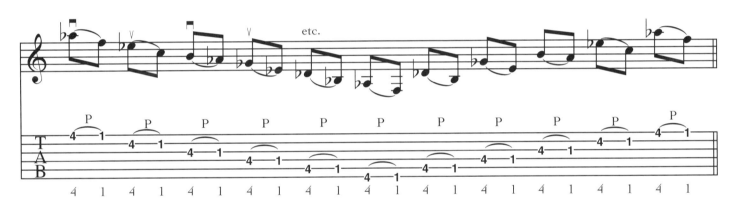

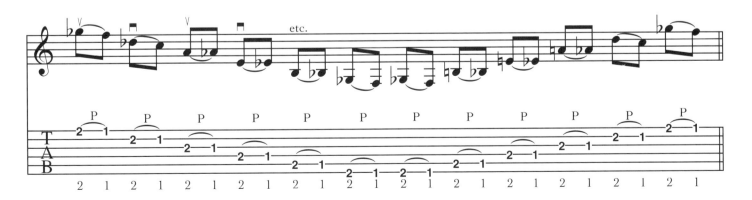

EXERCISE 58: 2ND TO 1ST FINGER PULL-OFFS

As with hammer-ons, you can pull-off more than one note at a time. This technique can be done very rapidly when mastered. Notice the alternate picking directions and be careful to dampen any ringing strings.

27.1   **EXERCISE 59:   E BLUES PENTATONIC PULL-OFFS IN TRIPLETS**

Just to keep you from getting too comfortable, this is Example #59 in 5th position with no open strings. This is more difficult but just as important.

27.2   **EXERCISE 60:   A BLUES PENTATONIC PULL-OFFS IN TRIPLETS**

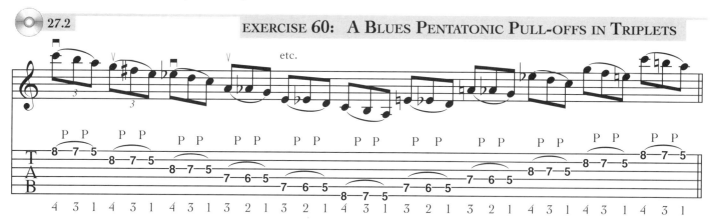

27.3   **EXERCISE 61:   E BLUES PENTATONIC PULL-OFF RIFF**

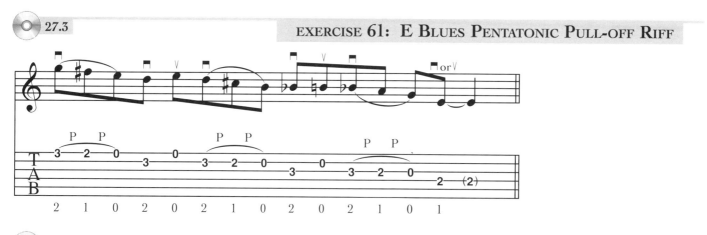

27.4   **EXERCISE 62:   A BLUES PENTATONIC PULL-OFF RIFF**

It is possible and desirable to do combinations of hammer-ons and pull-offs. Below are a few good exercises to get you going. Make sure that each note sounds clearly and at the same volume as all of the others. In all of these exercises, there is a finger pattern executed on one string that is then sequenced to all of the other strings. Each string is plucked only once, at the beginning of the pattern.

28.1   EXERCISE **63**: **2-4-2-1**

28.2   EXERCISE **64**: **3-4-3-1**

28.3   EXERCISE **65**: **1-2-3-4-3-2-1**

28.4   EXERCISE **66**: Cross-string Pull-off Pattern – **1-2-1-3**

This is a nice lick in D Harmonic Minor.

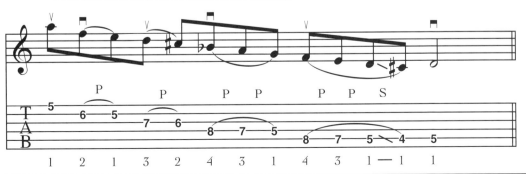

Chapter 3
Scale Combinations

In this chapter, we will start working on stretching, playing different finger patterns and moving up the fingerboard. The first set of exercises are scale combinations. You are going to play a C Major scale in 2nd position with no open strings in a pattern that goes like this:

Play the first three notes of the scale and return to the first note (1-2-3-1). Starting with the second note of the scale, again play three notes up—the second, third and fourth notes—and come back to the second (2-3-4-2); then 3-4-5-3. You get the idea. Melodically, this is called a *sequence*. The same melodic idea is repeated on different pitches.

Watch the fingerings very carefully. In this exercise, the symbol 1) in the fingerings means to extend your 1st finger out of its normal position on the 2nd fret to the 1st fret without moving your whole hand. It's a tough stretch but you can do it! And keep that alternate picking going strong.

29   **EXERCISE 67: C MAJOR SCALE IN COMBINATION 1**

Now that you have that one down, let's do the same exercise on a G Major scale. There are no extension fingers in this scale but it covers two octaves.

EXERCISE 68: G MAJOR SCALE IN COMBINATION 1

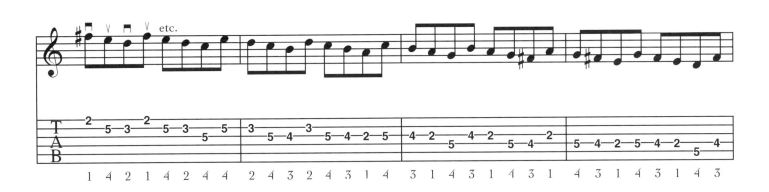

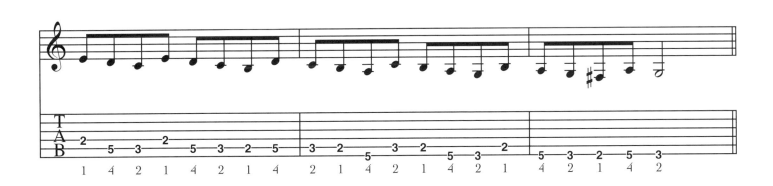

It should be no problem for you to do the same scale combination with the next three major scales. Just pay attention to the fingerings (and the notes!) and make sure you don't move your whole hand when you see 1) or 4). Just extend the 1st or 4th fingers out one fret more than usual.

31 EXAMPLE 69: A MAJOR SCALE—4TH FINGER, 6TH STRING

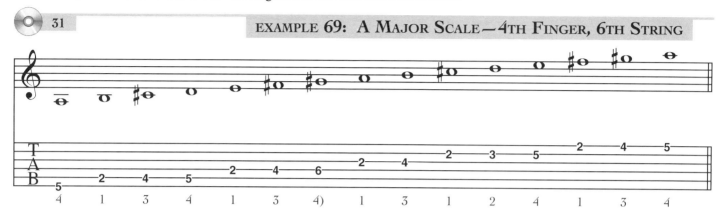

32 EXAMPLE 70: D MAJOR SCALE—4TH FINGER, 5 STRING

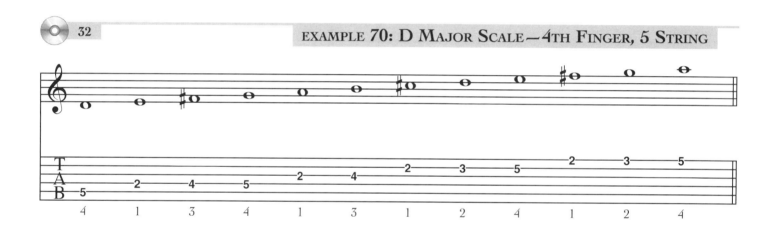

33 EXAMPLE 71: F MAJOR SCALE—1ST FINGER, 6TH STRING

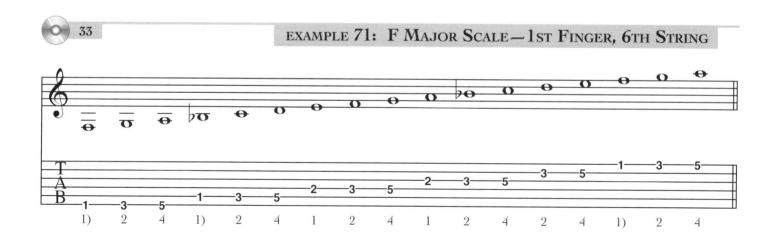

Now for something different: a new combination on a new scale. The combination is up four notes and back to the second, then start on the second note and go up four and back to the third, etc. (1-2-3-4, 2-3-4-5, 3- etc.)

We are going to do this combination on a G Dorian scale, which starts with your 1st finger on the 3rd fret G on the 6th string; in other words, in 3rd position. Watch out for those extensions with the 4th finger, marked 4). They can be tricky to get because the stretch is big. Go slowly and try to stay in position. Don't hurt yourself, but don't give up either.

Here is the G Dorian scale:

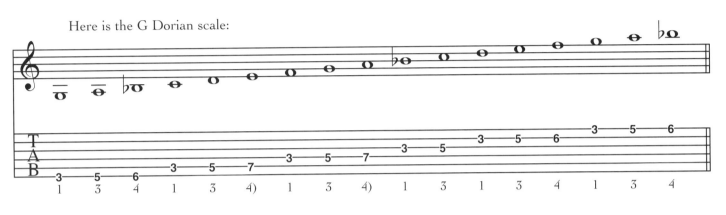

34 EXERCISE *72:* G DORIAN SCALE IN COMBINATION 2

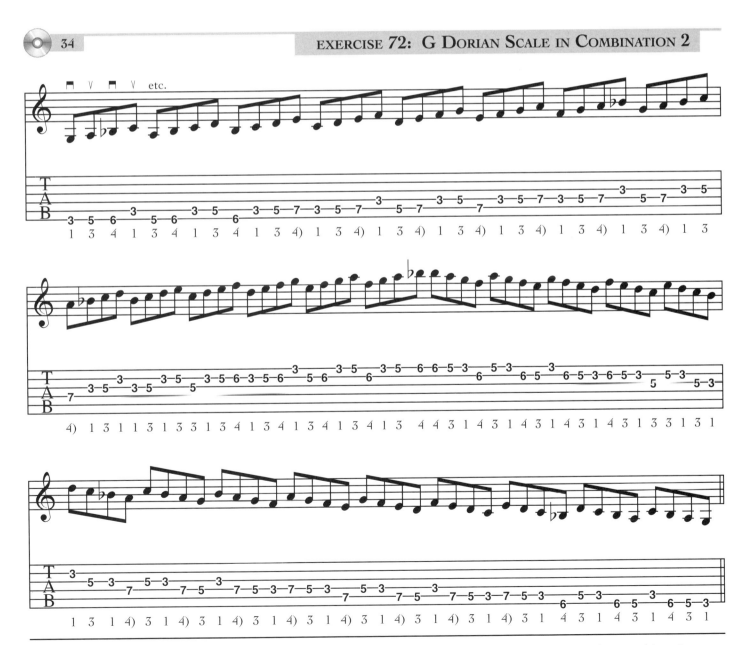

Going Up and Down the Fingerboard Quickly

We all want to do it, but how? Here are some really happening scales and arpeggios you can use to get up and down the fingerboard as fast as possible. The scale is called a *hexatonic* scale. It only has six notes instead of the usual seven. It has all but the fourth note of the major scale. Also, the fingering works out to be three-notes-per string. You have to play *very* accurately. The up side is that the fingering is always the same. The down side is that it is always 1 – 2 – 4, which is difficult. Try it first in triplets and then try it with straight eighths.

35.1

EXERCISE 73: THREE-OCTAVE F MAJOR HEXATONIC SCALE

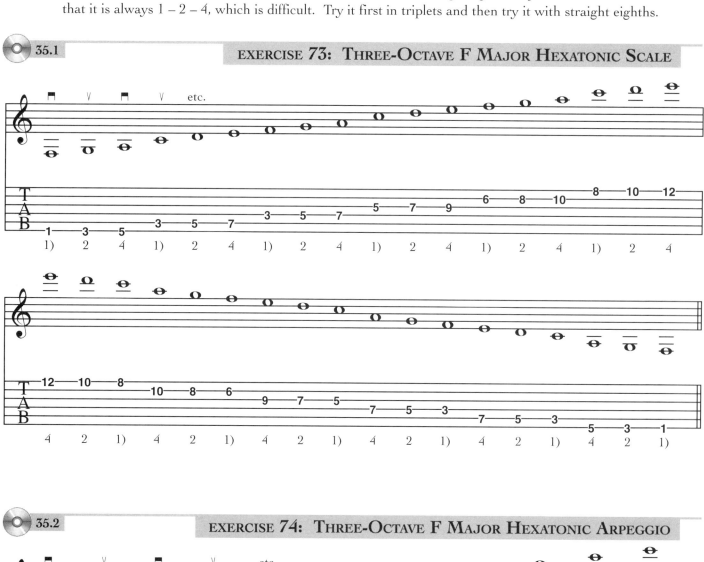

35.2

EXERCISE 74: THREE-OCTAVE F MAJOR HEXATONIC ARPEGGIO

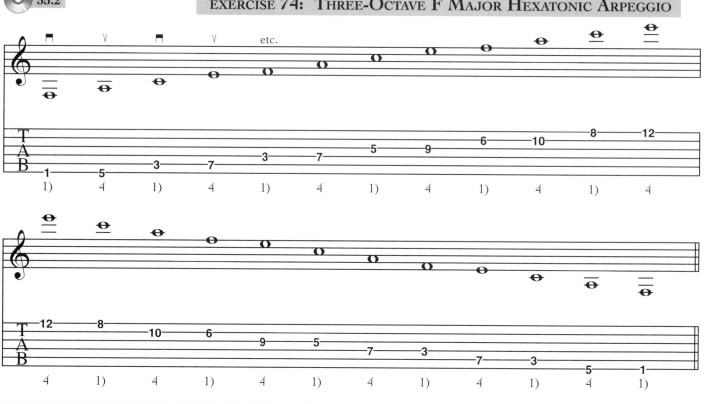

EXERCISE 75: THREE-OCTAVE G DORIAN HEXATONIC SCALE

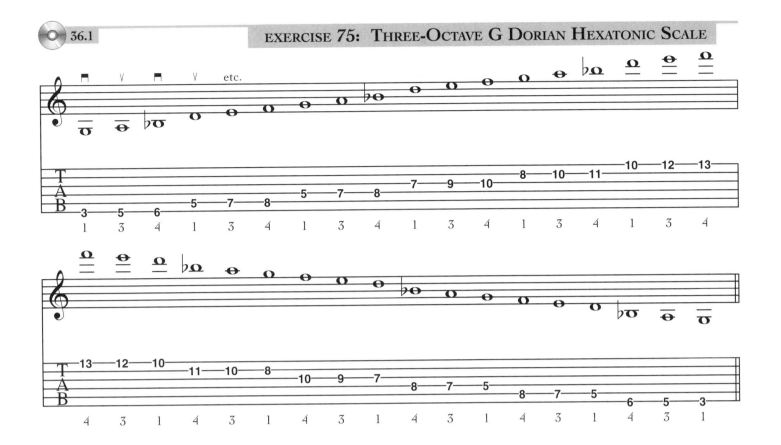

EXERCISE 76: THREE-OCTAVE G DORIAN HEXATONIC ARPEGGIO

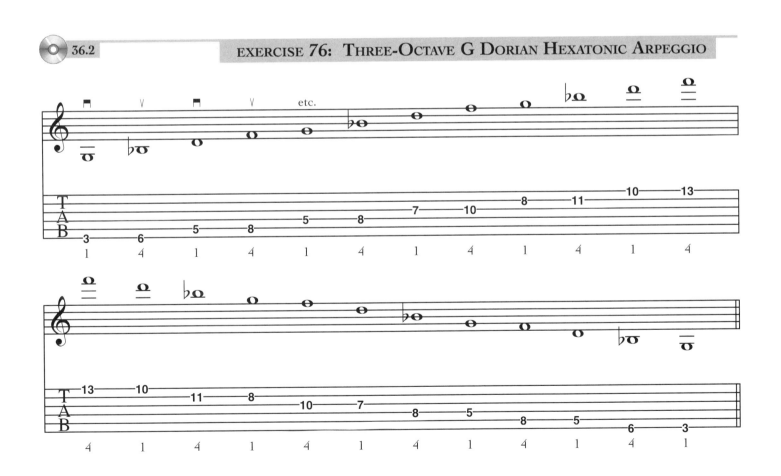

EXERCISE 77: THREE-OCTAVE A PHRYGIAN HEXATONIC SCALE

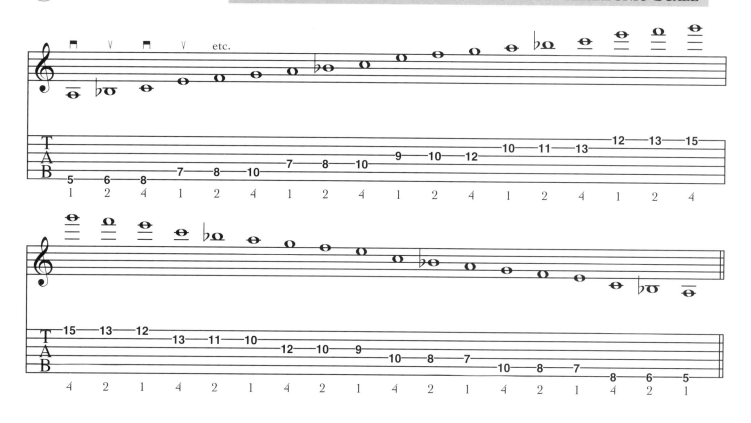

EXERCISE 78: THREE-OCTAVE A PHRYGIAN HEXATONIC ARPEGGIO

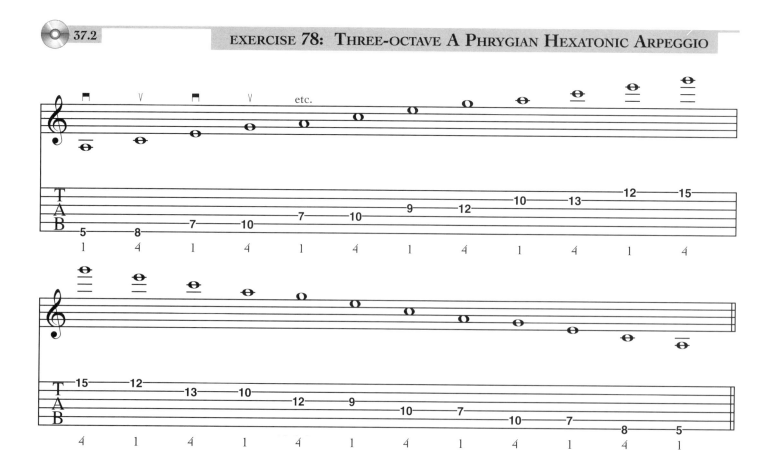

On page 19, we looked at sliding as a technique for moving smoothly up and down the fingerboard. The next two exercises use sliding and shifting positions as methods for traversing the fingerboard quickly and efficiently.

38.1   **EXERCISE 79: THREE-OCTAVE PENTATONIC MAJOR 3RD FINGER SLIDE**

In this exercise, the 3rd finger slides up to each G♯ and the final E. Put the 3rd finger on the string as you shift to the new position.

38.2   **EXERCISE 80: HALF-WHOLE DIMINISHED SCALE 1ST FINGER SLIDE**

This is a cool way to play the diminished scale up the fingerboard. The 1st finger slides up one half step (1-1-3-4). The fingering is consistent throughout.

Chapter 4

Cross Picking, String Skipping, Finger Rolls

This chapter is going to focus on exercises that will help you hone your *cross picking* (changing strings during alternate picking) and string skipping skills. You will still be using alternate picking in all of these exercises and there will even be some *finger roll* (playing two consecutive notes with the same finger on adjacent strings) techniques for you to learn.

Arpeggio Patterns

39.1

EXERCISE 81: MAJOR TRIAD TRIPLETS

This exercise outlines major triads in the cycle of 4ths starting with your 2nd finger on the 6th string. Remember to keep the alternate picking going no matter what!

39.2

EXERCISE 82: MAJOR 7 ARPEGGIOS

This one turns those triads into major *7 arpeggios* (broken chords). The first three and the fifth arpeggio in the series all start with a 1st finger note followed by a 2nd finger hammer-on. The fourth arpeggio has both a 1st finger slide and 1st finger roll. Go slowly and watch your hands carefully.

This exercise calls for alternate picking as you cross strings. The triplet rhythm will also challenge your alternate picking skills. Play slowly and strive for accuracy.

40.1   **EXERCISE 83: DIAGONAL EIGHTH-NOTE TRIPLETS**

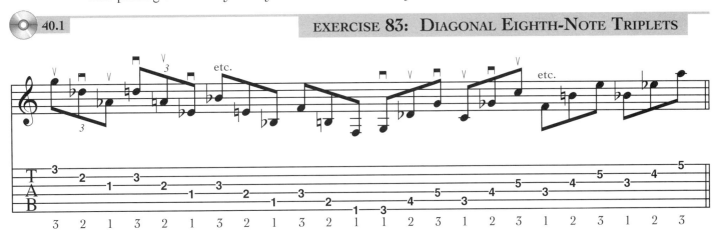

The next three exercises work on several things: alternate picking, moving up and down the fingerboard in a fluid manner, string skipping, triplet figures and legato technique. Don't rush. Perfect each exercise before moving on to the next.

40.2   **EXERCISE 84: THREE-OCTAVE F MAJ7 ARPEGGIO PATTERN**

This one has a lot of extensions with the 1st finger.

The ascending fingerings are given, but it's up to you to figure out the descending fingerings.

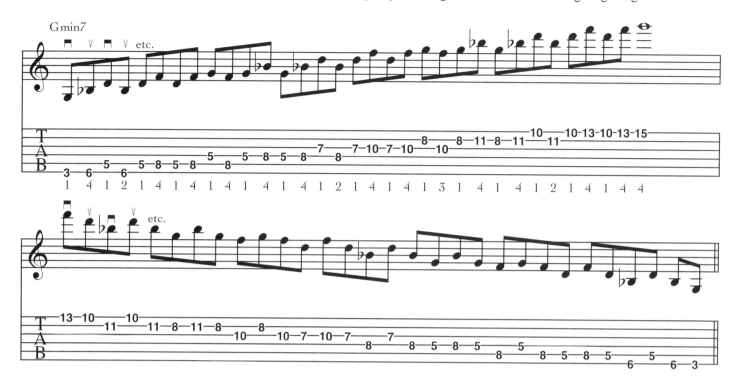

It's up to you to figure out the descending pattern and fingerings (as per Exercise 85).

Linkages are patterns which take you across the fingerboard from top to bottom or vice versa. Each linkage starts on a particular major scale degree from which four arpeggios are played one after another in descending or ascending order. You'll find that there are several instances where you have to "roll" one of your fingers across two strings to play two adjacent notes. Watch the fingerings and use alternate picking. Make sure you master these. You'll use them!

42.1   EXERCISE 87: MAJOR LINKAGE 1 FROM THE 2ND (OR 9TH) DEGREE

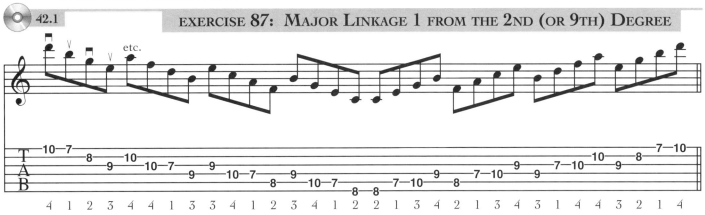

42.2   EXERCISE 88: MAJOR LINKAGE 2 FROM THE 7TH DEGREE

42.3   EXERCISE 89: MAJOR LINKAGE 3 FROM THE 5TH DEGREE

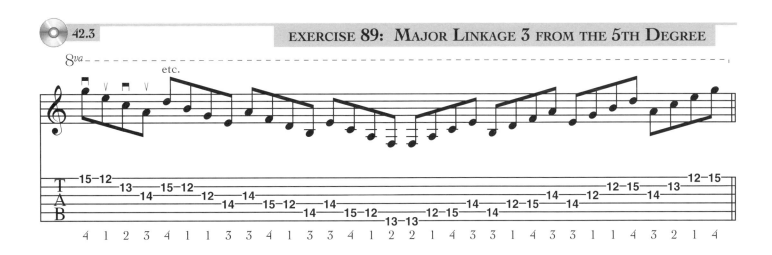

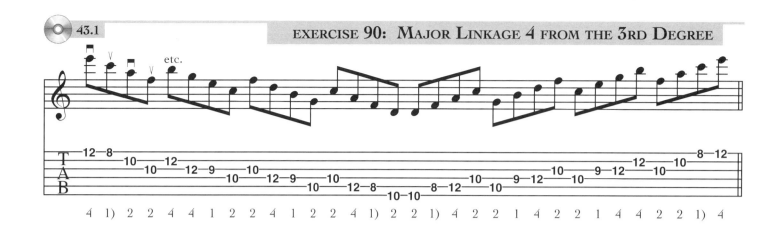

EXERCISE 90: MAJOR LINKAGE 4 FROM THE 3RD DEGREE

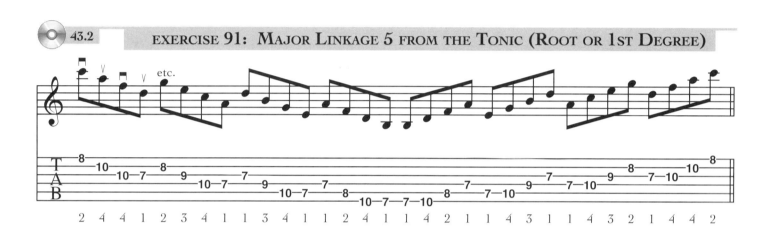

EXERCISE 91: MAJOR LINKAGE 5 FROM THE TONIC (ROOT OR 1ST DEGREE)

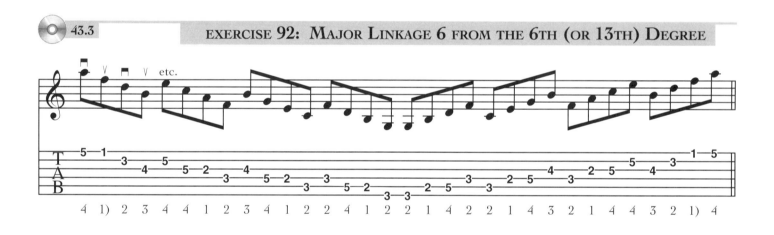

EXERCISE 92: MAJOR LINKAGE 6 FROM THE 6TH (OR 13TH) DEGREE

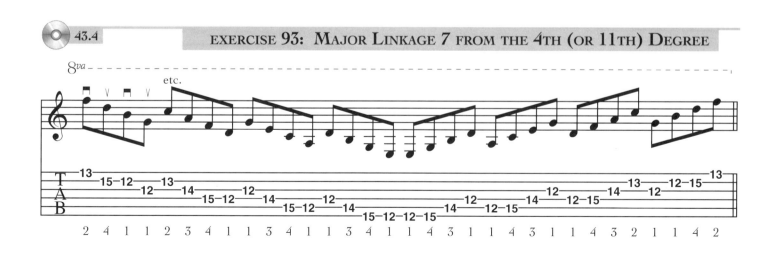

EXERCISE 93: MAJOR LINKAGE 7 FROM THE 4TH (OR 11TH) DEGREE

Arpeggiating 13th chords will give you exercise in several areas: 1) playing across all six strings from low to high; 2) cross picking, 3) playing triplets and 4) stretching.

If you arpeggiate a C Major 7 chord you get C, E, G and B played one at a time. You can add some kind of 9, 11 and 13 extension to any *diatonic* (from the key) 7 chord for color. These 13 arpeggios include the four notes in the chord plus a 9, 11 and 13. We'll ascend the fingerboard modally through F Major as eighth-note triplets and as straight eighths. These are very cool but tricky to grab if you don't go slowly at first. As usual, use alternate picking.

44.1   **EXERCISE 94: F MAJOR 13 ARPEGGIO**

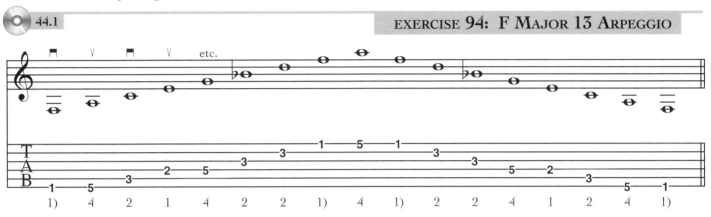

44.2   **EXERCISE 95: G DORIAN 13 ARPEGGIO**

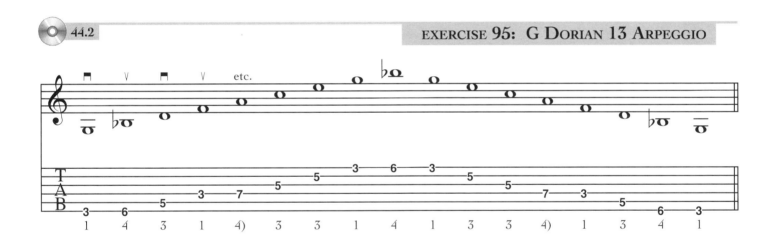

44.3   **EXERCISE 96: A PHRYGIAN 13 ARPEGGIO**

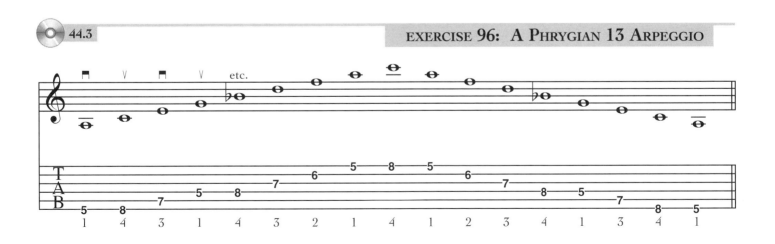

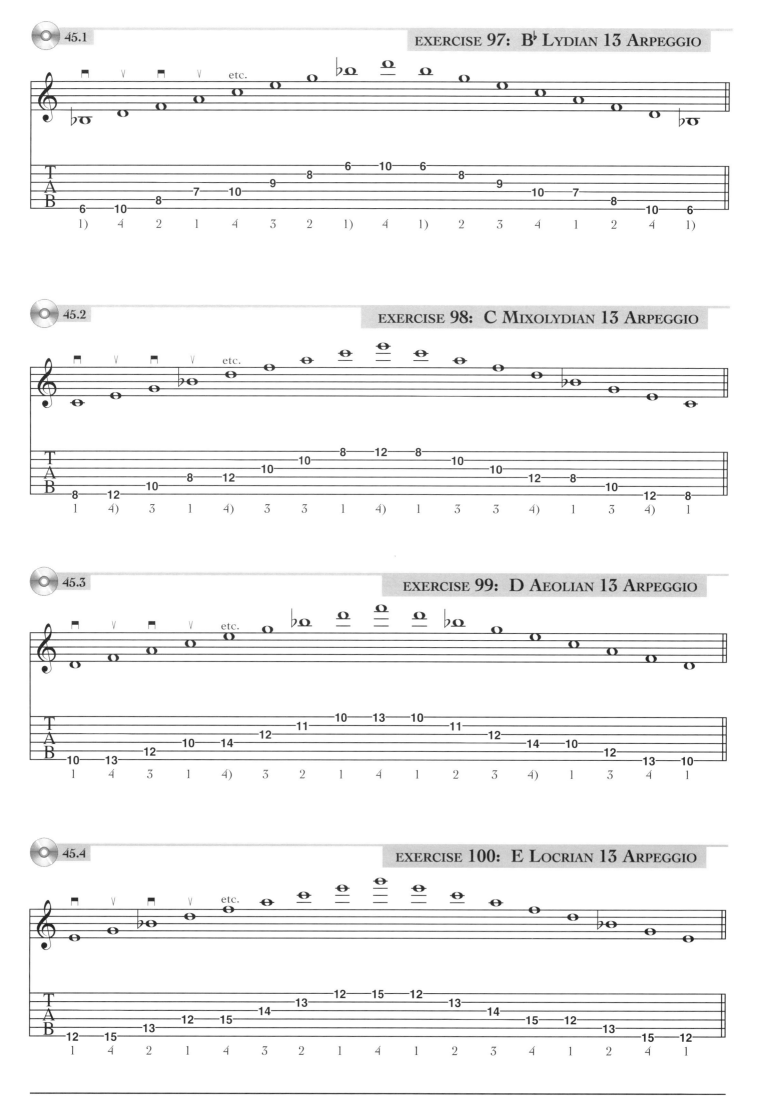

Chapter 5 — Sweeping, Rolling, Double Stops, Octaves

Sweeping Down

No, we're not talking about cleaning up your floors, although we could make an analogy about cleaning up—good articulation and efficient picking will result in clean playing. We've tackled a number of the problems you might be having with playing accurately, smoothly, efficiently and cleanly. Here's a new one: *sweeping*. Often, the solution to a rapid passage across adjacent strings is to pick in one direction with one long stroke. You can do this with downstrokes, upstrokes or a combination of both. The following exercises are typical jazz-style downstroke sweeps.

These are not "chords;" in other words, each note should sound by itself. Don't hold any notes down and allow them to ring while other notes are being played; rather, lift the left-hand fingers in sequence as each note is played. Follow the picking direction to the letter and you will gain new confidence in playing sweeping licks.

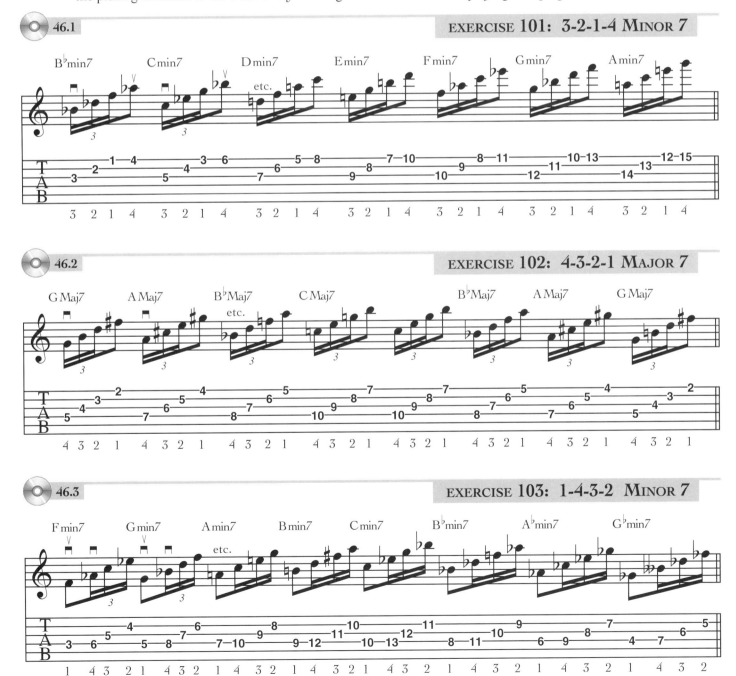

46.1 EXERCISE 101: 3-2-1-4 MINOR 7

46.2 EXERCISE 102: 4-3-2-1 MAJOR 7

46.3 EXERCISE 103: 1-4-3-2 MINOR 7

All of the chords on this page can be interpreted two ways.

EXERCISE 104: 1-4-3-2-1 MIN9/MAJ7

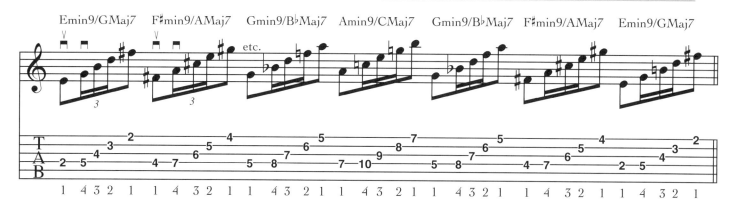

EXERCISE 105: 1-4-3-2-1-4 MIN11/MAJ 9

This exercise adds an upstroke on the very last note of each arpeggio. Try to make it the same volume as the rest of the sweep.

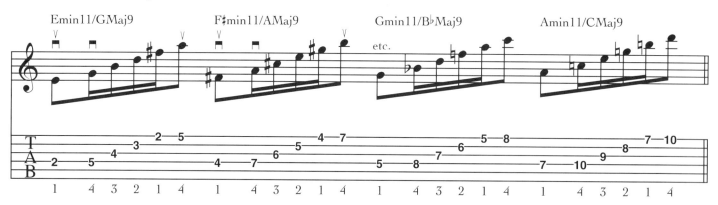

EXERCISE 106: 1-4-3-2-1 ii MIN7/V7

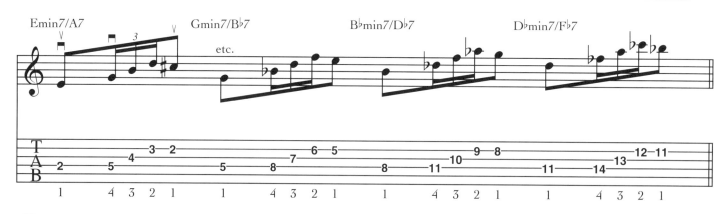

EXERCISE 107: 1-1-1-4 MIN9/MAJ7

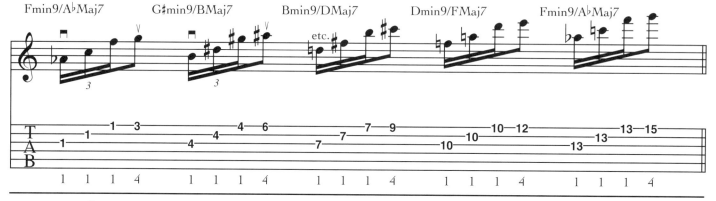

This exercise is a minor 7 sweep on the lowest three strings.

48.1   **EXERCISE 108: 1-4-3-1 MINOR 7**

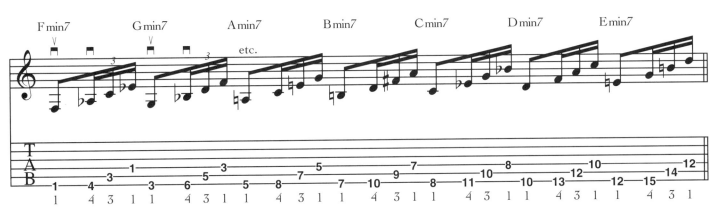

Two-in-a-Row Sweeps

These are somewhat tricky because you have to prepare for them. Make sure you have each one mastered before you try to combine them.

48.2   **EXERCISE 109: TWO MINOR 7 CHORD PATTERN**

Plant your left-hand fingers one at a time as you play the sweep. Don't try to set up all the fingers in advance of sweeping. It is all downstrokes except for the last note which is an upstroke. Have fun!

48.3   **EXERCISE 110: TWO-OCTAVE AUGMENTED TRIAD**

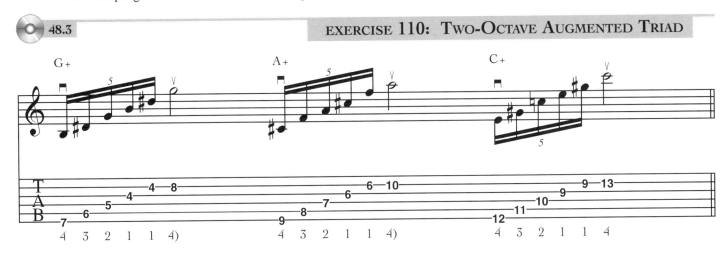

Sweeping up (using an upstroke) usually entails adding a downstroke on the very last note. Try this first exercise using a finger roll with the 2nd finger and ending on your 1st. Make sure we hear all four notes separately.

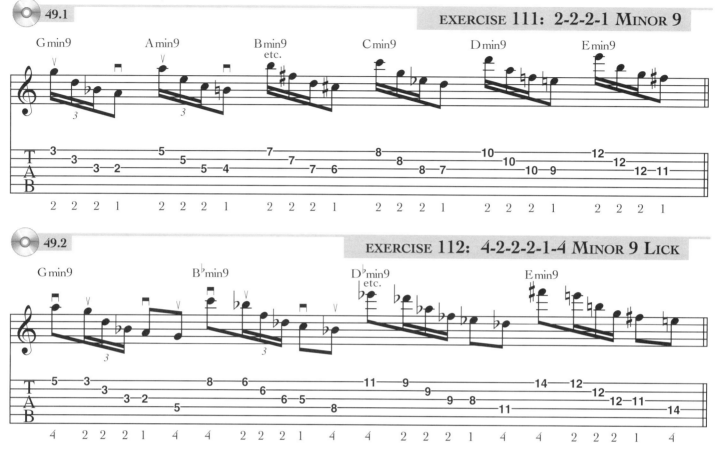

49.1 — **EXERCISE 111: 2-2-2-1 MINOR 9**

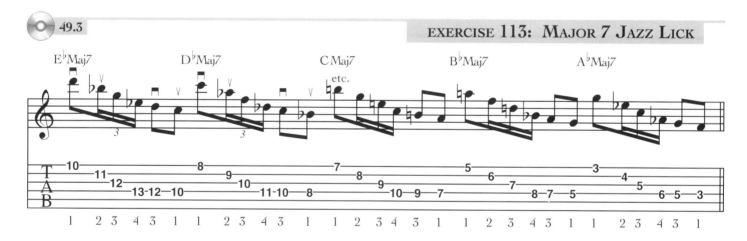

49.2 — **EXERCISE 112: 4-2-2-2-1-4 MINOR 9 LICK**

49.3 — **EXERCISE 113: MAJOR 7 JAZZ LICK**

49.4 — **EXERCISE 114: MAJOR TRIAD BLUES SWEEP**

The next two exercises will give you a crash course in how to "roll" your fingers across two strings in order to more smoothly play descending and ascending lines built on specific intervals. The idea is to plant your finger across two strings and, as you pick each string, slightly roll your finger from one to the other. Slightly means a very subtle move that is designed to eliminate having the two notes sounding together. These examples are built on 4ths and you will need to pay special attention to your alternate picking.

After mastering the exercise as written, try on all the other pairs of strings.

50.1   EXERCISE 115: 4THS ON THE TOP TWO STRINGS

50.2   EXERCISE 116: 4THS DESCENDING-ASCENDING LINE

50.3   EXERCISE 117: TRIPLET 4THS IN MINOR 3RDS

A *double stop* is two notes played together by one player. The first exercise is based on the familiar minor pentatonic scale.

51.1

EXERCISE 118: Minor Pentatonic Double Stops

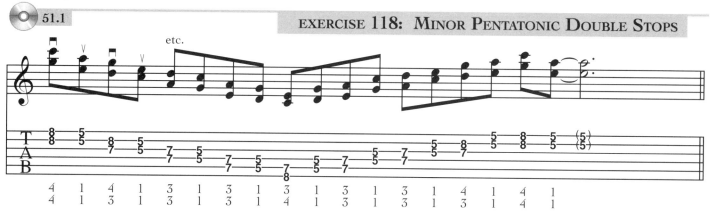

51.2

EXERCISE 119: Hexatonic Major 5ths and 4ths

This one is based on the F Hexatonic Major (no 4th degree) scale. The fingerings may seem awkward at first but follow them exactly and you'll be burnin'.

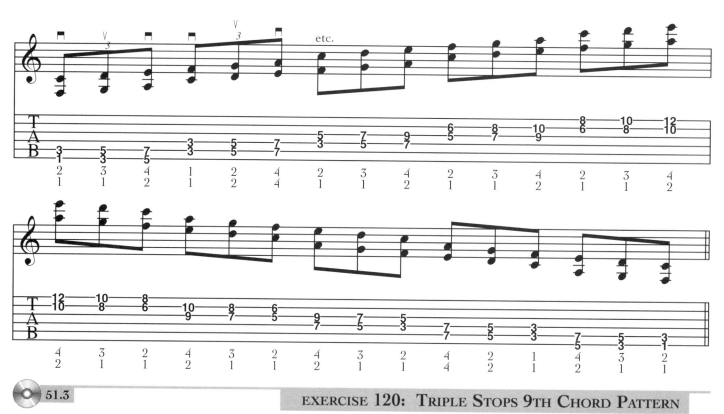

51.3

EXERCISE 120: Triple Stops 9th Chord Pattern

This exercise has three notes at a time—*triple stops*—in a pattern that moves down the fingerboard and across the strings in a very fluid, somewhat chromatic style. This example is in E.

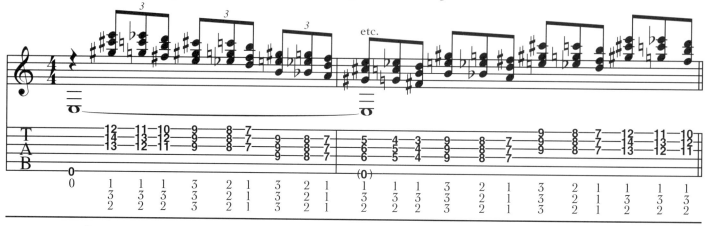

Octaves have been and still remain one of the most popular and cool ways to play in jazz guitar solos. There are several ways this can be done. The first thing to understand is that you will play octaves on pairs of strings that are not adjacent to one another. In other words, you would use the 1st and 3rd strings, or the 2nd and 4th strings, or the 3rd and 5th strings, etc. There is always a string between the two you are playing which has to be muted by your left hand.

This exercise calls for the 3rd/1st and the 4th/2nd string pairs played with the 1st and 4th fingers. Mute the string between the string pair with the side/bottom of the 1st finger. Notice that there is a four-fret spread between the left-hand fingers. This will occur whenever you play octaves on these pairs of strings.

52.1   EXERCISE 121: OCTAVES ON 3RD/1ST AND 4TH/2ND

52.2   EXERCISE 122: OCTAVES ON 5TH/3RD AND 6TH/4TH

Here's a similar exercise on the next two string pairs. The difference is that on these string pairs, you only have a three-fret spread. The fingering is up to you; either stay with the 1-4 or go to 1-3.

52.3   EXERCISE 123: SWITCHING OCTAVE SPACINGS

One of the trickiest aspects of playing octaves is handling lines that require you to switch from a four-fret spread (6th and 3rd or 4th and 2nd strings) to a three-fret spread (6th and 3rd or 4th and 1st strings).

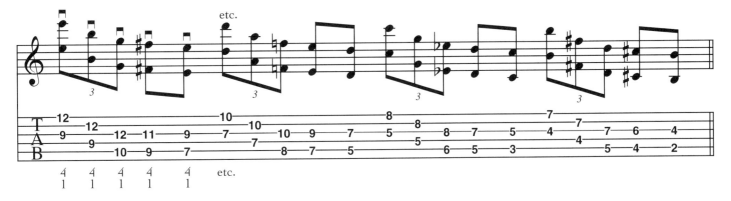

53.1

EXERCISE 124: LEAPS OF A MINOR 3RD IN OCTAVES

Now try some larger leaps with octaves.

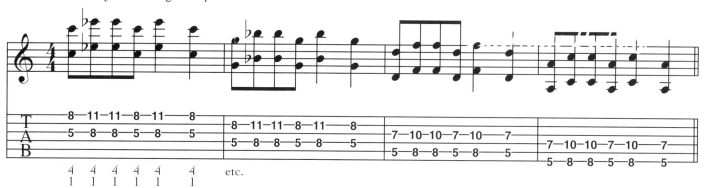

53.2

EXERCISE 125: OCTAVES IN THE STYLE OF WES MONTGOMERY

Now the question is whether to use a pick or your thumb like Wes Montgomery. Wes Montgomery would rest his fingers on the guitar while he used his thumb, and you can try that. It will give you some stability. Watch that thumb carefully because it is easy to accidentally hit unwanted strings.

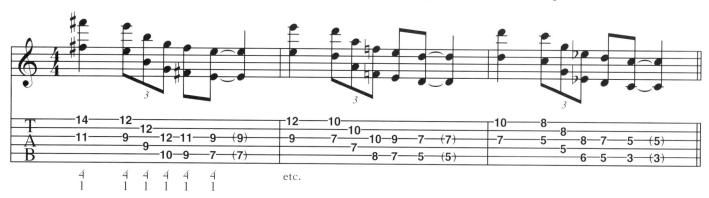

53.3

EXERCISE 126: PICK AND FINGER OCTAVES

Another way to play octaves involves the use of your pick and a finger at the same time in a plucking motion. Some people use their right-hand ring finger, but the middle can work also. This exercise uses the 5th and 2nd strings, and you'll notice that there are two strings between them, so pay special attention the muting.

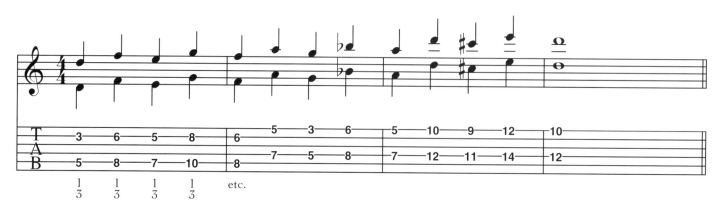

Chapter 6 — Chords

Playing chords can be tricky for several reasons: 1) the fingerings can be difficult; 2) the fingerings must be memorized; 3) they require putting the fingers down all at once and 4) we must be able to switch from chord to chord smoothly and in tempo.

The following exercises will teach you harmonized major scales on different sets of strings. Memorize them. Learn to put all your fingers down at once and always look for *anchor fingers* – fingers that you can keep on a string during a chord change. Read the diagrams in these exercises from left to right. Practice each one slowly until you can play it smoothly and with confidence. Then, work on increasing the tempo.

 54.1   **EXERCISE 127: HARMONIZED MAJOR SCALE, SET 1—6, 4, 3 AND 2**

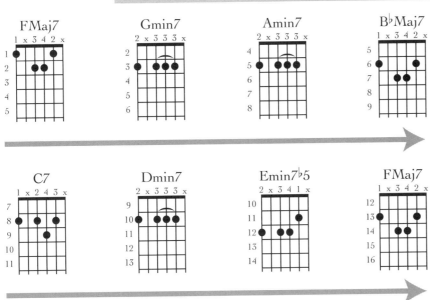

 54.2   **EXERCISE 128: HARMONIZED MAJOR SCALE, SET 2—5, 4, 3 AND 2**

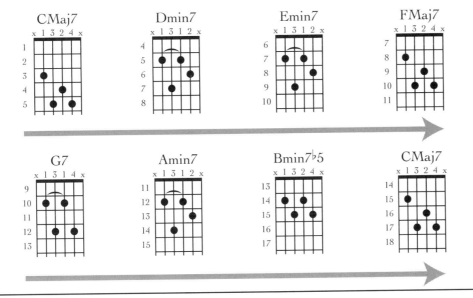

EXERCISE 129: HARMONIZED MAJOR SCALE, SET 3—4,3,2 AND 1

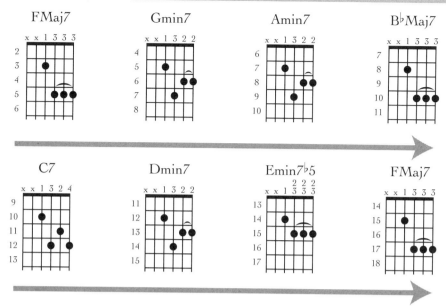

EXERCISE 130: HARMONIZED MAJOR SCALE, SET 4—6,5,4 AND 3

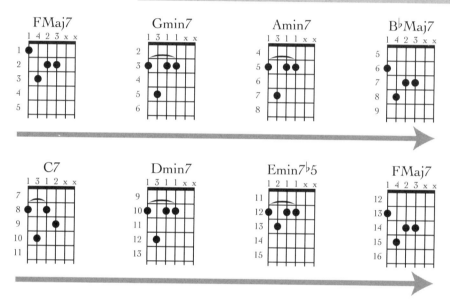

So far, our chords have all been in *root position*, meaning that the root has been the lowest note in every chord. In the following two exercises, the 5th of the chord is the lowest note. We call this *5th in the bass* or *2nd inversion*. Play slowly! Notice the 4th finger anchor.

EXERCISE 131: HARMONIZED MAJOR SCALE—2ND INVERSION SET 1

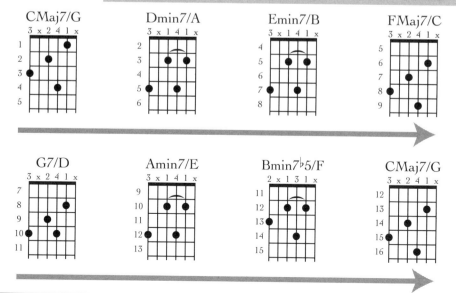

EXERCISE 132: HARMONIZED MAJOR SCALE—2ND INVERSION SET 2

FMaj7/C

Gmin7/D
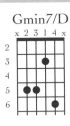

Amin7/E
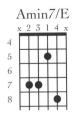

B♭Maj7/F
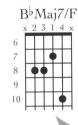

C7/G

Dmin7/F
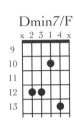

Emin7♭5/B♭
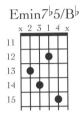

FMaj7/C
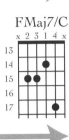

The next two exercises are in *1st Inversion*. The 3rd of each chord is the lowest note.

56.2

EXERCISE 133: HARMONIZED MAJOR SCALE—1ST INVERSION SET 3

CMaj7/E
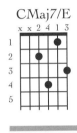

Dmin7/F
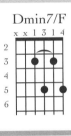

Emin7/G

FMaj7/A

G7/B
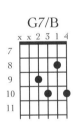

Amin7/C
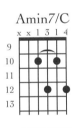

Bmin7♭5/D
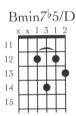

CMaj7/E
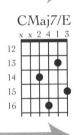

56.3

EXERCISE 134: HARMONIZED MAJOR SCALE- 1ST INVERSION SET 1

FMaj7/A
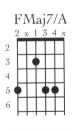

Gmin7/B♭
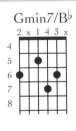

Amin7/C
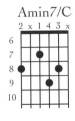

B♭Maj7/D
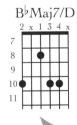

C7/E
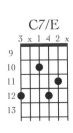

Dmin7/F
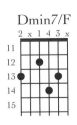

Emin7♭5/G
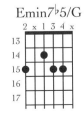

FMaj7/A
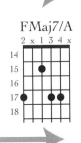

Now let's focus on anchor fingers. The following exercises all have at least one finger that remains on the fingerboard on its string even though you are changing chords and changing position. Keep 'em down.

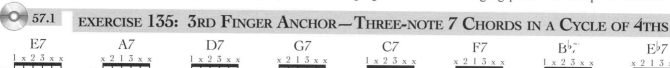

EXERCISE 135: 3RD FINGER ANCHOR—THREE-NOTE 7 CHORDS IN A CYCLE OF 4THS

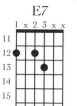 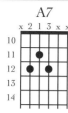  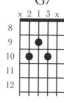 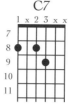 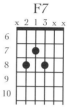 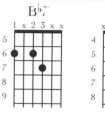 

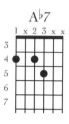 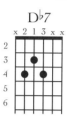 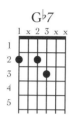 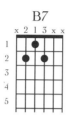 

EXERCISE 136: 4TH FINGER ANCHOR—MAJOR 7 CHORDS IN A CYCLE OF 4THS

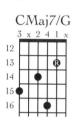 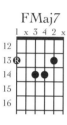 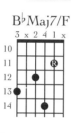 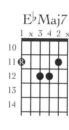 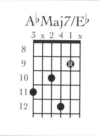 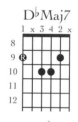

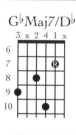  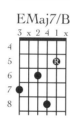  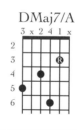 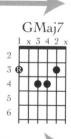

EXERCISE 137: 1ST FINGER ANCHOR—ii MIN9 TO V9 IN A CYCLE OF 4THS

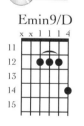 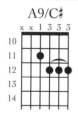 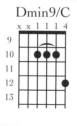 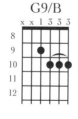  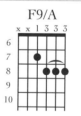

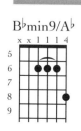 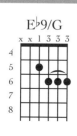 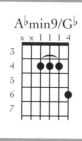 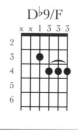  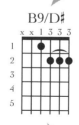

The following exercises have more than one anchor finger. Keep them on their strings as you change chords.

58.1   EXERCISE 138: 1ST AND 3RD ANCHOR FINGERS—CHORDS (13 TO 9) IN A CYCLE OF 4THS

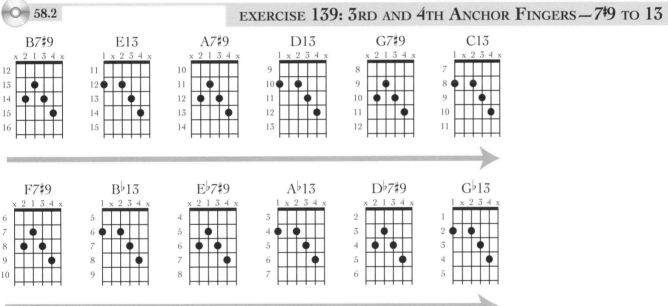

58.2   EXERCISE 139: 3RD AND 4TH ANCHOR FINGERS—7♯9 TO 13

58.3   EXERCISE 140: ALL 4 FINGERS—ii MIN11 TO V7♭5/♭5 CHROMATIC BASS

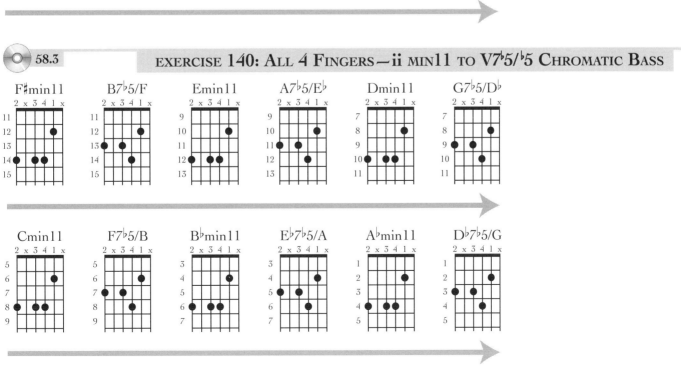

Shifting is changing positions. With a lot of practice, this becomes easy. The trick is to practice your shifts accurately and with ease repeatedly so that accuracy and ease become the habit.

There are various shifts you will see repeatedly in jazz tunes, so here are a few of the most common chord shifts to practice:

59.1   EXERCISE 141: ii MIN9-V7♭9-I6/9 — 1ST FINGER ANCHOR

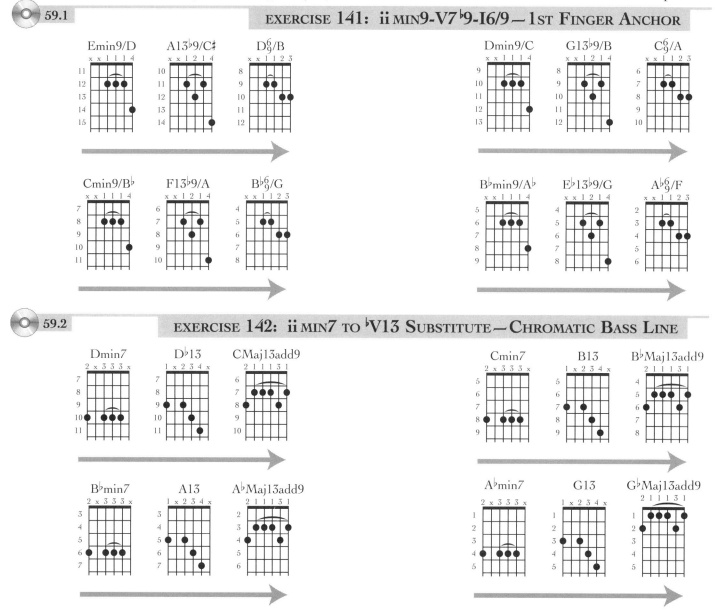

59.2   EXERCISE 142: ii MIN7 TO ♭V13 SUBSTITUTE — CHROMATIC BASS LINE

There are three sets of fingerings for this exercise…do all three just like the first one. Fortunately, the fingerings don't change during each exercise.

59.3   EXERCISE 143: ii MIN9 TO V13♭9 — 1ST FINGER ANCHOR

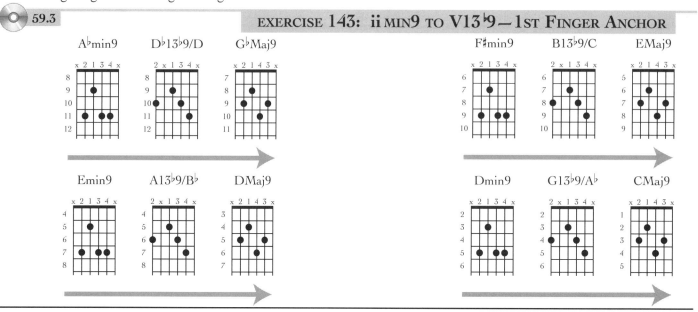

EXERCISE 144: SHIFTING ii-V-I

Amin7/G · Amin9/G · Cmin9/B♭ · Cmin7/B♭

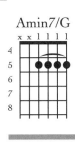 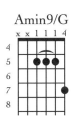 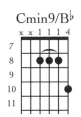 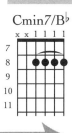

D13♭9/F♯ · D7♭9/F♯ · G6/9

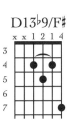 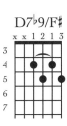 

EXERCISE 145: ANOTHER SHIFTING ii-V-I

Dmin11 · Emin11 · F6/9/A · G6/9/B

 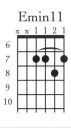 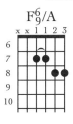 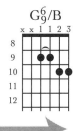

Dmin9/C · G13♭9/B · C6/9/A · C6/9/E

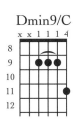 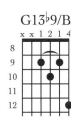 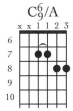 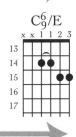

EXERCISE 146: I7-VI7-II7-V7 TURNAROUNDS

This is a cool way to play a I7-VI7-II7-V7 turnaround: approach each chord from a half step above.

G7 · F7 · E7 · B♭7 · A7

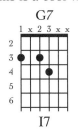 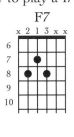 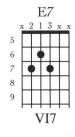  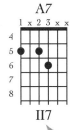

I7 · VI7 · II7

E♭7 · D7 · A♭7 · G7

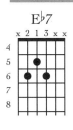 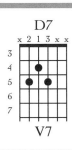 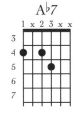 

V7 · I7

There are plenty of chord *voicings* (a voicing is the arrangement of notes in a chord) that demand large stretches in the left hand. Here are some exercises to help you become accustomed to these distances. Practice slowly. Make sure that each note is sounding clearly. If you can't perform a stretch well in the lower positions of the fingerboard, move it up to a higher position where you can do it (the frets are closer together in the higher positions) and work your way down. Also, in the lower parts of the fingerboard, you might have to bring your thumb down to the bottom edge of the fingerboard in order to get more distance with your fingers. And you might even have to lean your fingers towards the headstock.

 61.1

EXERCISE 147: MIN9 TO MIN7 — THE TOP THREE STRINGS

These chord forms will work throughout this exercise.

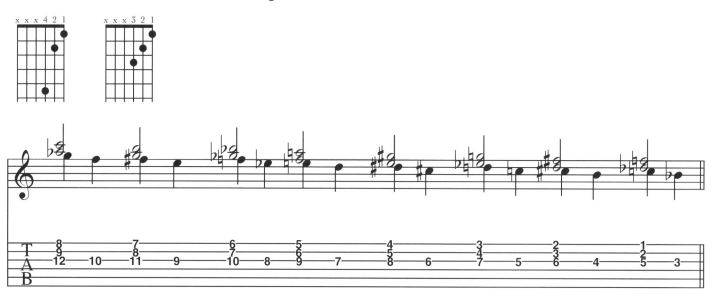

 61.2

EXERCISE 148: MIN9 TO MIN7 — THE TOP FOUR STRINGS

These chord forms will work throughout this exercise.

EXERCISE 149: CLOSE VOICINGS ON THE TOP FOUR STRINGS

In a *close voicing*, all the notes of a chord are as close together as possible. The three chord forms below will work throughout this exercise.

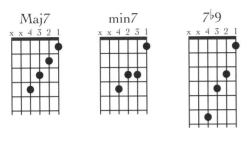

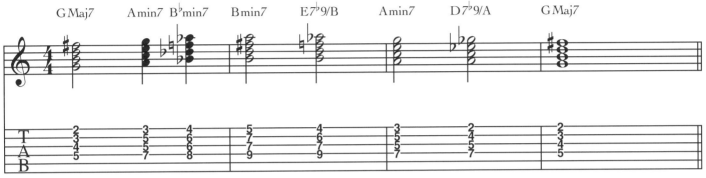

EXERCISE 150: IV/V-V9-V7♭9-IMAJ7

The chord forms on the left will work for each progression below.

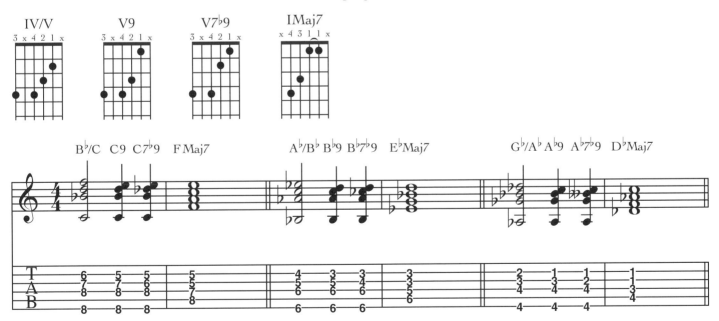

EXERCISE 151: ii MIN7-♭II 13ADD9-I MAJ7

These chord forms will work for each of the progressions below.

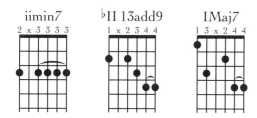

iimin7   ♭II 13add9   IMaj7
2 x 3 3 3   1 x 2 3 4 4   1 3 x 2 4 4

Bmin7   B♭13add9   AMaj7   Amin7   A♭13add9   GMaj7   Gmin7   G♭13add9   FMaj7

EXERCISE 152: ii MIN7-V9

These chord forms will work for each iimin7-V9.

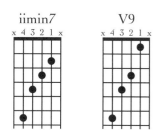

iimin7   V9
x 4 3 2 1 x x 4 3 2 1 x

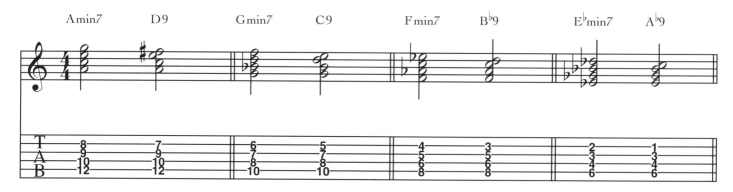

Amin7   D9   Gmin7   C9   Fmin7   B♭9   E♭min7   A♭9

Chapter 7 — Comping

Comping is the art of accompaniment. And make no mistake—it is an art. There are lots of right-hand techniques, lots of different grooves, many kinds of moving lines and voice leading, etc.

Four to the Bar

Let's start with the standard four-beats-to-a-bar groove, all downstrokes in the style of Freddie Green. This is a very powerful groove and it goes with the ride cymbal perfectly. First, make sure you know the chord voicings provided.

 64.1   EXERCISE 153: QUARTER-NOTE DOWNSTROKES

Use the second min7 chord below for the min7 chord that falls between the two 7♭9 chords in the progression.

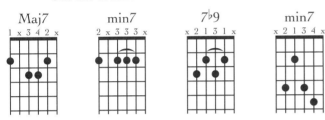

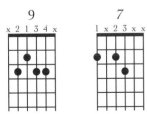 64.2   EXERCISE 154: QUARTER-NOTE DOWNSTROKES WITH HALF-STEPS

One thing you can do to spice up 153 is to walk or slide into some of the chords from a half step away, either above or below. Plus, you can put in a little subtle upstroke every once in a while.

Now try playing the bass note first, then the rest of the chord. Play the bass note with a downstroke and the rest of the chord with an upstroke. This will make you sound like you are playing two parts at once…which you are!

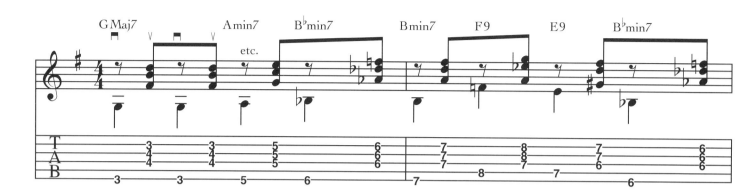

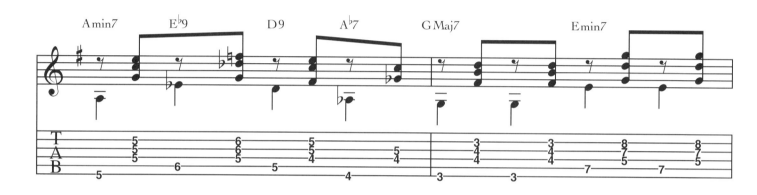

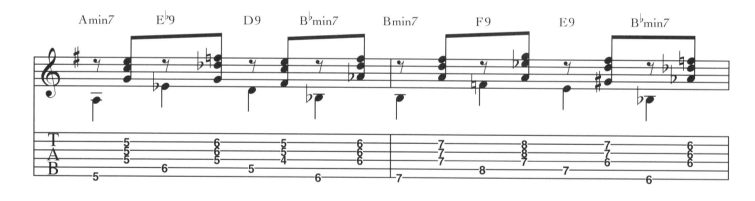

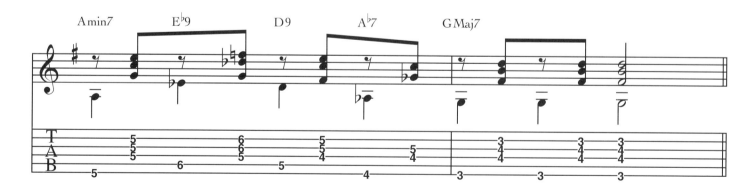

Continuing in the same vein as on page 52, we can learn a new technique to enable us to more easily play the preceding examples: *pick and fingers*. As the name implies, you use the pick (*pk*) for the bass notes and your *m*, *a* and *c* fingers for the other notes of the chord. The tricky part comes when you switch string sets—you have to move your right hand to the new set. The real upside is that you will end up with a bass line that totally swings.

Right-Hand Fingers

pk	=	Pick
m	=	Middle
a	=	Ring
c	=	Pinky

66

EXERCISE **156:** PICK AND FINGERS

Two-Note Voicings

In some styles, it is necessary to play a different chord on every single beat. One way to do this is to play smaller voicings, such as three-note or even two-note voicings. This works because you only need the 3rd and the 7th of a chord to define the chord harmonically. The next exercise is a series of ii-V-I progressions that illustrate the two-note idea. Try downstrokes.

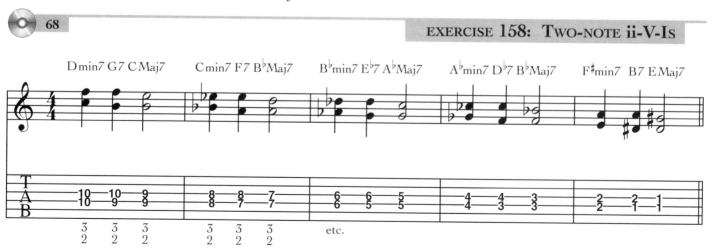

The next step is to try three-note voicings. Here is a twelve-bar blues comping pattern with one chord per beat.

69

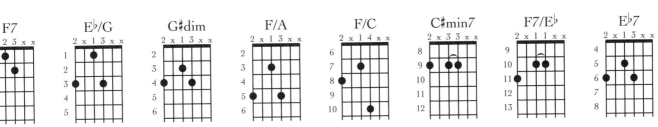

EXERCISE 159: THREE-NOTE BLUES

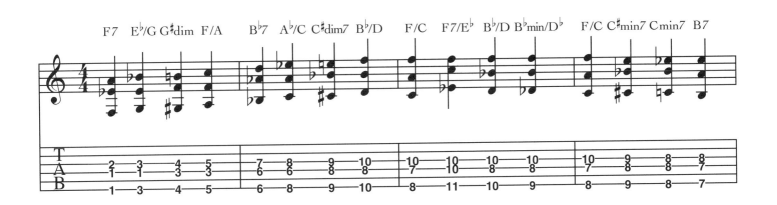

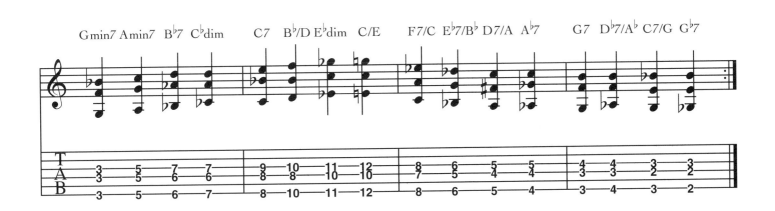

In *parallel motion*, each note in the chord moves in the same direction, the same number of steps when changing from one chord to the next. In other words, the fingering doesn't change but the position of the chord does.

 70.1

EXERCISE 160: BLUES PARALLEL MOTION

Take a look at this section of a blues. Learn the given chord voicings before trying the example.

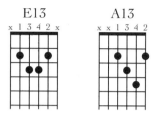

In *contrary motion,* notes move in opposite directions during a chord change. For example, the bass line might descend as a melody line ascends.

 70.2

EXERCISE 161: CONTRARY MOTION

Check out these chord voicings first:

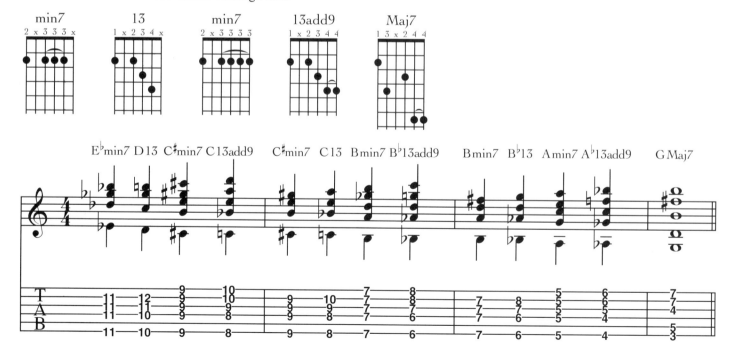

A *counter line* is a secondary melodic line played within chord changes, "against" or at the same time as the main melody of a tune.

71.1

EXERCISE **162:** COUNTER LINE INSIDE

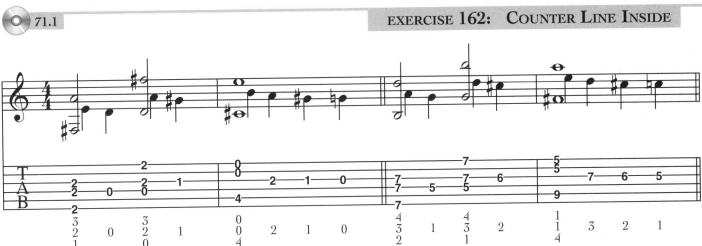

Another nice idea is the use of a *common note* or *common tone* to tie together a group of chords.

71.2

EXERCISE **163:** COMMON TONE

Notice the F on the 6th fret of the 2nd string. This note is in every chord of this example. It behaves like a *pedal tone* (a tone that remains the same as harmonies change beneath or above it).

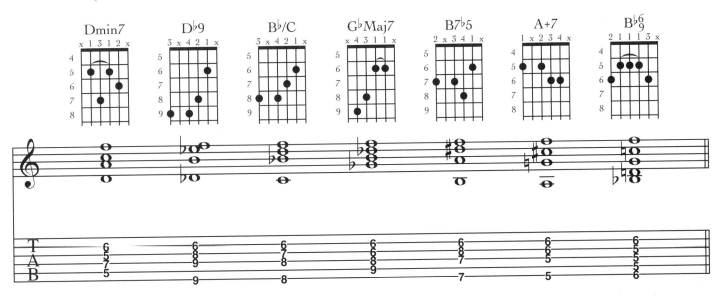

EXERCISE 164: COMMON TONE WITH DESCENDING BASS LINE

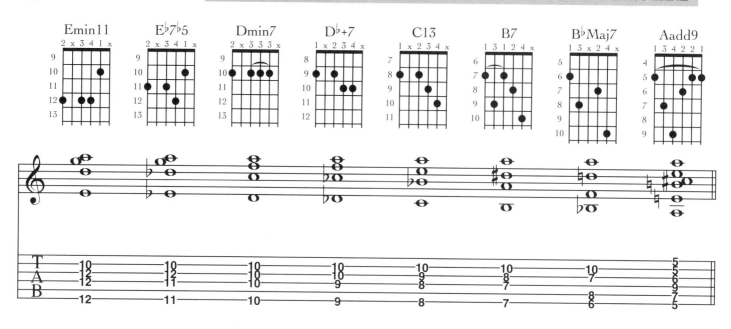

Pedal Tones

We touched on pedal tones in Example 163 on page 69. The idea is that one note remains the same while you change chords around it. It can be a bass note, a middle note or a top-note. Here are three E top note pedals and one G pedal:

EXERCISE 165: BLUES TURNAROUNDS WITH HIGH-E AND HIGH-G PEDALS

EXERCISE 166: BLUES TURNAROUND WITH CONTRARY MOTION

EXERCISE 167: BLUES TURNAROUNDS WITH LOW-E PEDAL

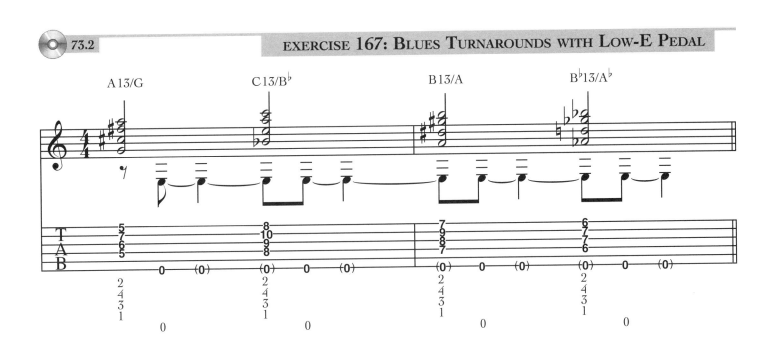

Another way to play chordal accompaniments is *fingerstyle*. Get rid of the pick completely (for now) so that you can use your entire hand. There are lots of possibilities in terms of which string to play, in what order, how loud, etc. In the following exercises we are going to try to show you as many of them as we can. Keep in mind that these are for your picking hand—usually the right hand—so we will use the same chord progression each time.

74.1   **EXERCISE 168: FINGERSTYLE MAJOR CHORD SCALE IN C**

The first exercise is simply to pluck four-note block chords with four fingers. Your thumb is on the 5th string, your index finger is on the 4th, your middle finger is on the 3rd and your ring finger is on the 2nd string.

74.2   **EXERCISE 169: MAJOR CHORD SCALE IN C—THUMB & FINGERS**

Now, pluck with the thumb first, then with the fingers.

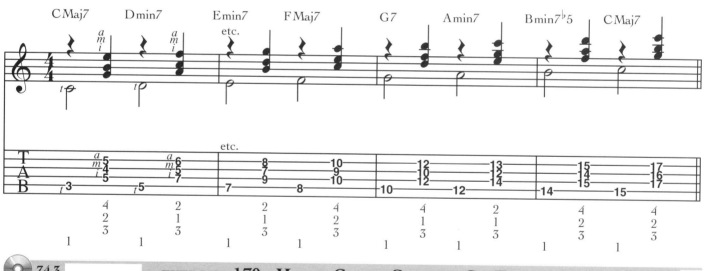

 74.3   **EXERCISE 170: MAJOR CHORD SCALE IN C—THUMB, 1ST/2ND & 3RD**

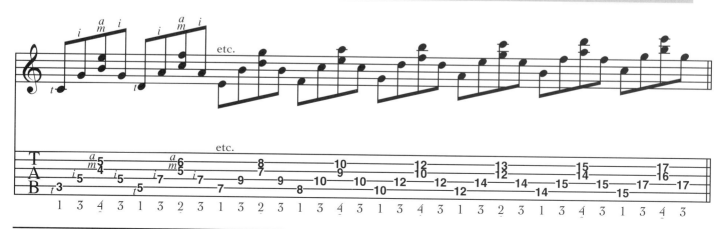

Try this one evenly as written and then as a very fast roll, one finger after another.

EXERCISE 171: MAJOR CHORD SCALE IN C—T - I - M - A

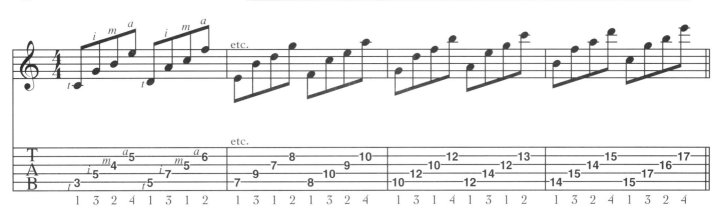

EXERCISE 172: MAJOR CHORD SCALE IN C—SIXTEENTH-NOTE TRIPLETS

EXERCISE 173: MAJOR CHORD SCALE IN C—TWO AGAINST THREE

Separating the thumb and fingers makes it possible to play two different rhythms simultaneously. Your thumb plays straight quarter notes while your fingers play quarter-note triplets above. Just for fun, we'll change the progression to a set of descending iimin7/$\flat$II13s.

These chord voicings are used throughout the exercise.

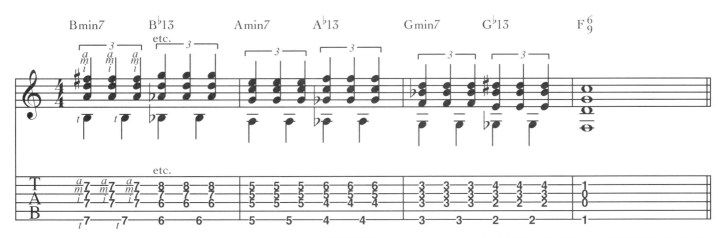

Using harmonics in a piece can create a dazzling effect. But the technical execution is tough because you have to be delicate, exact with both hands and your articulation has to be perfect. Let's start with an exercise using *natural harmonics*, the ones found on the open strings. Make sure that your left-hand finger barely touches the string directly above the fret itself, the actual steel wire, not in the middle between two frets.

 78.1   EXERCISE 174: NATURAL HARMONICS—5TH AND DOUBLE OCTAVE

The harmonics in this exercise are found on the 5th and 7th frets. Pluck firmly and remove your left-hand fingers quickly so that they don't hinder the free vibration of the strings. Hold down the bass note with your 1st finger or 2nd finger and play the harmonics with another finger, usually the 4th or 3rd. Try a pluck and a fast roll with your right hand.

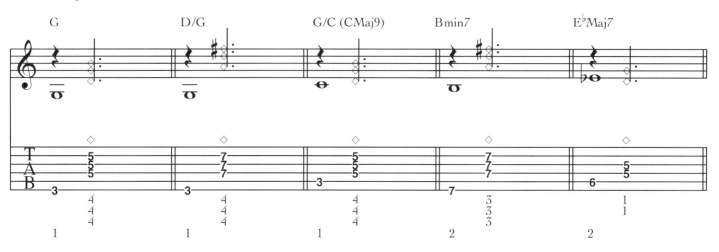

 78.2   EXERCISE 175 – ARTIFICIAL HARMONICS: 5TH, DOUBLE OCTAVE AND 3RD

It is possible to create harmonics on notes that are being fingered. These are called *artificial harmonics*. Here's the logic: You can use your right hand to touch the string above a fret twelve (or five or seven) frets higher than the note you are fingering. It probably works best to touch the string above the appropriate fret with the outstretched index finger while your thumb plucks the string underneath the hand. This technique takes lots of practice but is worth the work. In this exercise, barre the 5th fret and touch the string just above the 17th fret (5th fret plus 12 frets = 17th fret).

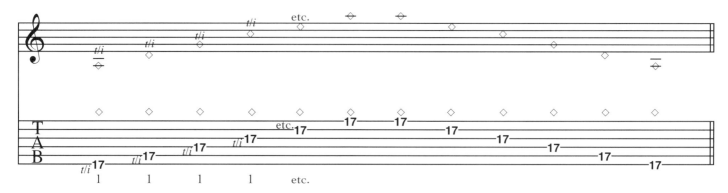

EXERCISE 176 – MIXING ARTIFICIAL HARMONICS WITH NORMAL NOTES

In this exercise, play the open 4th string with your right-hand ring finger (*a*) and follow it with a harmonic on the 12th fret of the 6th string. Then play the open 3rd string with your ring finger and follow it with a harmonic on the 12th fret of the 5th string played with the artificial harmonic technique (right-hand only). Continue in this manner.

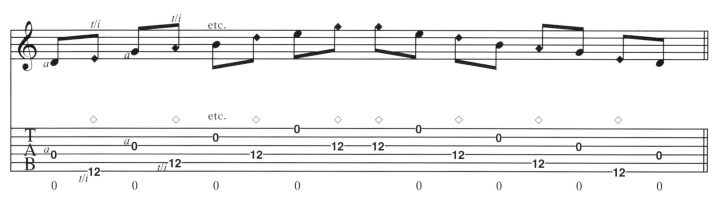

EXERCISE 177 — ARTIFICIAL HARMONICS ON 1ST-FINGER BARRE

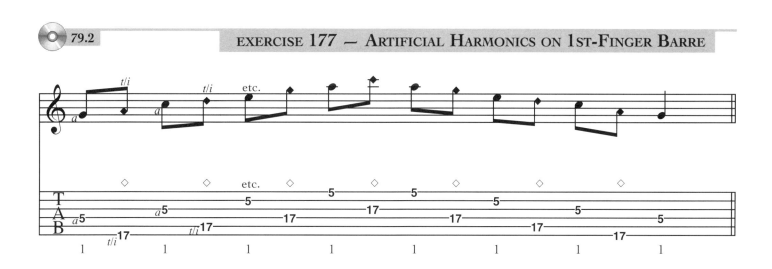

EXERCISE 178 — ARTIFICIAL HARMONICS ON THE MAJOR PENTATONIC

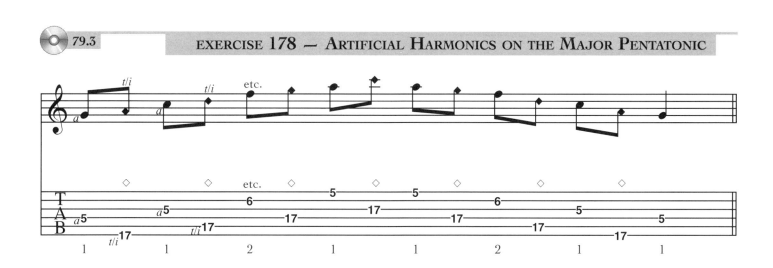

EXERCISE 179 – ARTIFICIAL HARMONICS ON C9

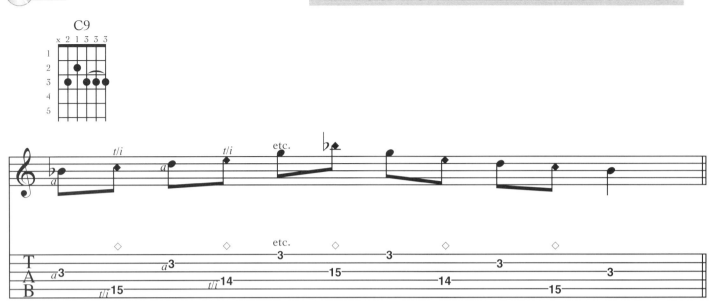

EXERCISE 180 – ARTIFICIAL HARMONICS ON E9

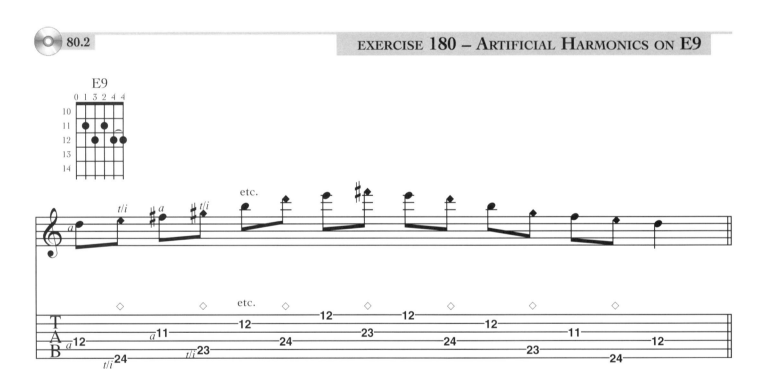

This exercise is really fun to play! First play through the chord voicings so that you have all the fingerings mastered before you begin.

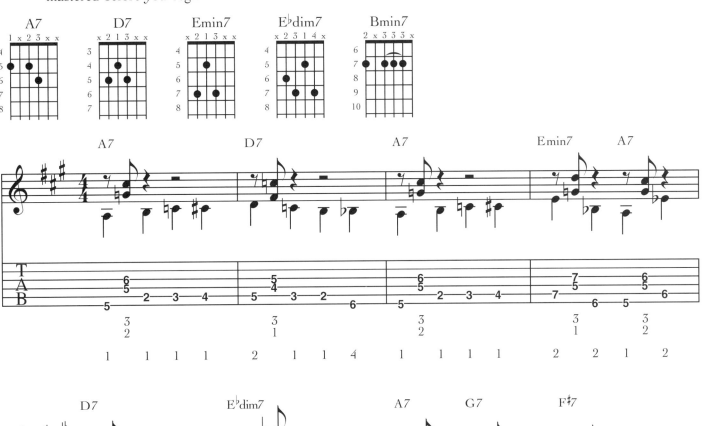

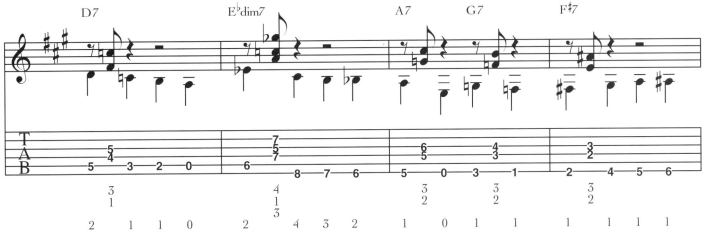

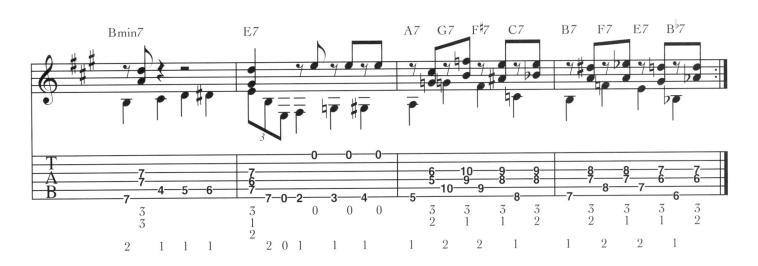

The chord progression called *Rhythm Changes* comes from the song, *I Got Rhythm*, from George Gershwin's "Porgy and Bess." It has been used in many different songs, including lots of Charlie Parker tunes. It is important to know these changes a few different ways. Try playing them with a pick, pick and fingers and just fingerstyle. Use walking bass lines and anything else you can think of to make it happen and, by the way, they are almost always in B♭.

 82   **EXERCISE 182: RHYTHM CHANGES**

LEAD SHEET

You can either read the standard lead sheet chart below or the chord diagrams in the chord chart beginning below (from left to right) beneath it. Have fun—you've earned it! Play the chords in order as written, then mix and match!

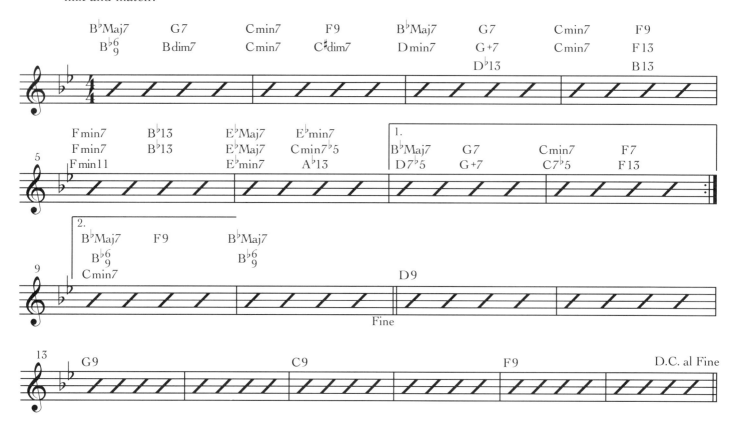

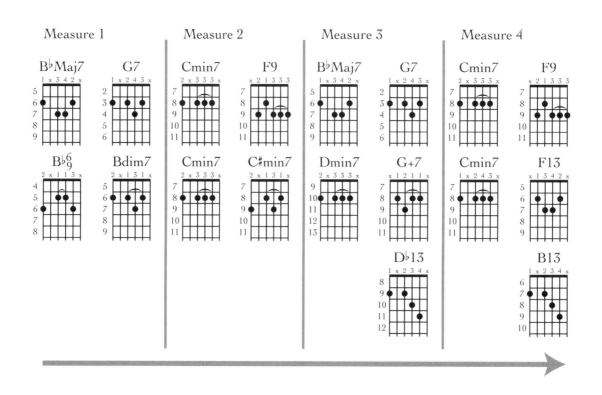

Measure 1   Measure 2   Measure 3   Measure 4

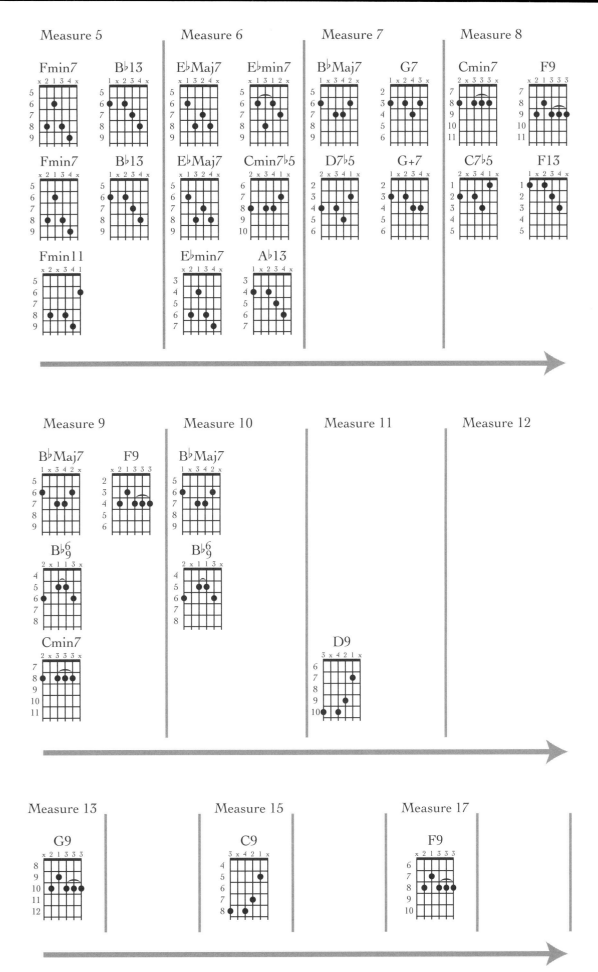

Measure 5   Measure 6   Measure 7   Measure 8

Measure 9   Measure 10   Measure 11   Measure 12

Measure 13   Measure 15   Measure 17

Congratulations! You've made it all the way through *Jazz Chops* at least once. We hope that you have found this book to be helpful and will to continue to use the exercises to improve your technique. Make sure to find practical uses for some of the licks and chord forms in the exercises. Remember, becoming a good jazz player is a life-long process, something that evolves over time and with a lot of practice and playing experience. For further information, be sure to check out the many other titles from The National Guitar Workshop, especially the jazz books including *Stand Alone: Jazz, Jazz for the Rock Guitarist, Chord Connections, The Complete Jazz Guitar Method* and *Jazz Skills*. Enjoy!